To Verona

God Bless you &

keep the faith

Jeffrey Bohanno

5-5-06

God's Folks

A Proper Perspective
for Peculiar People's
Pathway to Perseverance

JEFFREY T. BOHANNA

authorHOUSE®

AuthorHouse™
1663 Liberty Drive, Suite 200
Bloomington, IN 47403
www.authorhouse.com
Phone: 1-800-839-8640

First published by AuthorHouse 4/21/2008

ISBN: 978-1-4343-8198-9 (sc)

Printed in the United States of America
Bloomington, Indiana

This book is printed on acid-free paper.

This book is dedicated to my loving wife, Taminka, and our four wonderful children (Jakyla, Jessica, Jada, and JaNya). As well as to my dearly departed parents, Louella Bohanna and Delane Shaw. To my wonderful family as a whole and to the greatest congregation in the world, Terry Street Church of Christ. To my Father in the Gospel, Lee Otis Smith, Sr.. Last but not least, to the Mighty God of Heaven, His Christ, and His Holy Spirit.

CONTENTS

INTRODUCTION

IT IS A TRUE ASSESSMENT that no one loves the idea of being defeated, at least no one in a competent state of mind. Now if one is saddened by defeat, it becomes an amazing spectacle, to see one defeat themselves. I'm persuaded to think that God never intend for man to be fun of the idea of pain, but somehow, some people in this life have created within themselves a high tolerance for hurt. Now astonishing as that idea is, it's even more devastating to see the people of God affect themselves with this *disease* called "self defeat." Now if you think that the word disease is too strong a word to use here then consider the following idea:

Disease is defined as a disorder of structure or function in a human, animal, or plant, especially one that produces specific symptoms. In other words, when someone or something has a disease there will be evidence of the disease seen in that person or thing. Now in like manner, when those who have confessed their faith in Jesus, allow themselves to be defeated by the ills of this life, then there will be evidence of that defeat seen in that person. What makes the self-defeat of a Christian so closely related to a disease is the fact that a disease breaks down the nature and normal order of a Christian and the defeat is visibly seen by all. The normal and natural order of a Christian is that we are victorious. Paul says in I Cor. 15: 57, "*But thanks be to God, which giveth us the victory through our Lord Jesus Christ.*" Another allegory to this idea is that self-defeat is contagious, just as most diseases. Thus that old saying, "misery loves company." Most of the time when one has defeated themselves, they will most likely want to bring someone else into their pity party and not only that, but they would even dare to bring down the whole house, you know that one bad apple thing.

When I consider the thought of a child of God giving up, giving in to defeat, I often wonder what is on the mind of God, as He looks down on his children and see so many of them living beneath their potential. Potential is defined as *having the capacity to develop into something in the future., qualities or abilities that may be developed and lead to future success or usefulness.* Since God has put potential in each of us, I wonder if He is gnashing His teeth at the fact that some of His children are not allowing themselves to see the possibilities of a prosperous, plentiful, and productive life that ALL of His children can have. I even now wonder, do some of us in the Lord's church believe in the eternal Godhead's ability. I say that because if we truly believe, then the question becomes why do some of us continue to struggle day after day. Think of the idea that we belong to the God that owns a cattle on a thousand hills, the God that is responsible for life itself and yet some of us in the Lord's church have a problem with paying our bills. Now don't get me wrong here, I'm not just speaking of finances, but defeat as a whole. Whether it's financial, emotional, spiritual, or domestic, all of us in the house of God should be able to <u>show some evidence that God can and will take care of His own.</u> If the majority of the saints who have been washed in the blood of the lamb continue to struggle, then how could we convince anybody else that they need to be a Christian. God's folks must realize that we cannot continue in self-defeat. The same truth that David spoke in Ps 37 : 25, still holds to this day in the 21st century. David says, *"I have been young, and now am old; yet have I not seen the righteous forsaken, nor his seed begging bread."*

For a good example of this, let's look back at Israel's self-defeat:

(Joshua 2 : 1 - 11) *Now Joshua the son of Nun sent out two men from Acacia Grove to spy secretly, saying, "Go, view the land, especially Jericho." So they went, and came to the house of a harlot named Rahab, and lodged there. And it was told the king of Jericho, saying, "Behold, men have come here tonight from the children of Israel to search out the country." So the king of Jericho sent to Rahab, saying, "Bring out the men who have come to you, who have entered your house, for they have come search out all the country." Then the woman took the two men and hid them. So she said, "Yes, the men came to me, but I did not know where they were from. And it happened as the gate was being shut, when it was dark, that he men went out. Where the men went I do not know; pursue them quickly, for you may overtake them." (But she had brought them up to the roof and hidden them with the stalks of flax, which she had laid in order on the roof.) Then the men pursued them by the road to the Jordan, to the fords. And as soon as those who pursued them had gone out, they shut the gate. Now before they lay down, she came up to them* on the roof, and said to the men: "I know that the LORD has given you the land, that the terror of you has fallen on us, and that all the inhabitants of the land are fainthearted because of you. **For we have heard** how the LORD dried up the water of the Red Sea for you when you came out of Egypt, and what you did to the two kings of the Amorites who were on the other side of the Jordan, Sihon and Og, whom you utterly destroyed. **And as soon as we heard these things, out hearts melted; neither did there remain any more courage in anyone because of you, for the LORD you God, He is God in heaven above and on earth beneath.**

Now watch the self-defeating aspect of this passage as it relates to God's Folks, Israel. Forty year earlier Moses, in Numbers 13 : 1 - 2, was command by God to send spies down to the land of Canaan to spy out the land. Once the spies went down and saw the inhabitants and saw that there were giants in the land, they became discouraged and in the mist of their discouragement watch what happened next and notice how the affection spread through out all the camp of God's people. Numbers 13 : 31 - 33: *But the men who had gone up with him said, "We are not able to go up against the people, for they are stronger than we." And they gave the children of Israel a bad report of the land which they had spied out, saying, "The land through which we have gone as spies is a land that devours its inhabitants, and all the people whom we saw in it are men of great stature. There we saw the giants(the descendants of Anak came from the giants); and we were like grasshoppers in our own sight, and so we were in their sight,"*

Now watch this, all the inhabitants in Canaan had already heard about Israel and their God according to Rahab in Joshua 2 : 10 -11. It turns out that had

Israel went into Canaan, despite the large inhabitants, when Moses had sent the spies to spy out the land, they could have easily taken what God had already given to them(Numbers 13: 2). They had the victory, but they defeated themselves. Rahab said that, " *And as soon as we heard these things, our hearts melted; neither did there remain any more courage in anyone because of you, for the LORD your God, He is God in heaven above and on earth beneath.*" Now if that isn't profound enough, then look at it from this light. By the time these spies come over and converse with Rahab it is forty years later. Forty years ago, God's folks could have been in a place better than the one they were in; but because of their reprehensible mind set, they defeated themselves. *For forty days they spied and for forty days they denied, so for forty years they strived and at the end of forty years, they died.* An old preacher said once, "What it took forty years to do, could have been done in less than two."

So what was God's folks(Israel) problem? How did they defeat themselves so easily, even after they had been delivered from bondage? Here's what happened:

GOD'S PROPERTY

The first of their problems was that they, somehow, could not conceive in their mind that they were **God's Property**. When Israel was encapsulated by Egyptian bondage, God told Moses through a bush that burned in Exodus 3: 7 - 10, how he had heard the cry of his people. Notice the language God used, "*And the Lord said, I have surely seen the affliction of my people which are in Egypt, and have heard their cry by reason of their taskmasters; for I know their sorrows; And I am come down to deliver them out of the* hand of the Egyptians; for I know their sorrows; And I am come down to deliver them out of the hand of the Egyptians, and to bring them up out of that land unto a good land and a large; unto a land flowing with milk and honey; unto the place of the Canannites, and the Hittites, and the Amorites, and the Perizzites, and the Hivites, and the Jebusites. Now therefore, behold, the cry of the children of Israel is come unto me: and I have also seen the oppression wherewith the Egyptians oppress them. Come now therefore, and I will send thee unto Pharaoh, that thou mayest bring forth **my people**, the children of Israel out of Egypt." Could you imagine physically and visually seeing the hand of God moving in your favor, to bring you out of hundreds of years of slavery and oppression just as He did for the people of Israel? So the only conclusion that I can arrive at is that Israel somehow could not fully comprehend that they belonged to God. At the time they spied out Canaan, if they had been fully cognizant of whom they belonged to, they would have gone in and taken what was theirs. They were in fact **God's Property.**

GREATER POSITION

Secondly, since they could not fully comprehend that they were God's Property, they also could not conceive that there was a Greater Position waiting for them than the one they were in and most of all than the position they came out of in Egypt. Watch what they had the audacity to say to Moses after they returned from spying out Canaan. Numbers 14 : 1 - 4, "So all the congregation lifted up their voices and cried, and the people wept that night. And all the children of Israel complained against Moses and Aaron, and the whole congregation said to them, "If only we had died in the land of Egypt_ Or if only we had died in this *wilderness_ Why has the LORD brought us to this land to fall by the sword, that our wives and children should become victims? Would it not be better for us to return to Egypt? So they said to one another,* **"Let us select a leader and return to Egypt."** Their self-defeat caused them to believe that death was better than what God had promised and that their position in Egypt was better than the position that God had prepared for them. One of the most strongest and most powerful saying I have ever heard was the one that said, "If you don't stand for something, you'll fall for anything." God's folks must realize that none of us have to settle for less. If God can't produce a good life for his children, after we have went through the "wildernesses of life", the holy mandates of scripture are a collection of lies. However, I believe the words of Paul as he writes to Titus in <u>Titus 1: 2, God cannot lie. So if the problem isn't with God, then guess who it's with?</u> There was a greater position for Israel and there is a greater position for you.

GRASP THE POSSIBILITIES

Thirdly, Israel's problem was that, they could not *Grasp the Possibilities*. Since they could not fully see that they were God's Property, and since they could not perceive that they could have had a Greater Position, all because they fail to Grasp the Possibilities of being in that Greater Position. I heard it said once that <u>if you believe it, you can achieve it.</u> Looking at Israel I can easily see the opposite of that saying, if you don't believe it, you won't achieve it. Some of the people of Israel somehow didn't believe that God could do in Canaan, what he did in Egypt. Some of us are mirror images of Israel. God has blessed us in many areas of our life, yet for some reason we act as if there are some things in this life too hard for God. With awe-inspiring authority God asked Abraham in Gen. 18 : 14, "Is anything too hard for the Lord?" The same God that brought us out of the miry clay of life's oppressive fights, is the very same God that can deliver us from whatever else life has to throw our way. Certainly, I hope that none of us think that our successes in which lead us to where we are today is because of what we did for ourselves. Moreover, along the same lines, many of us have not seen much success, because of our own failure to grasp the possibilities of God doing greater things in our life.

GRASSHOPPER PERSONALITY

Finally, the reason Israel couldn't fully conceive that they were God's Property, and the reason they could not visualize being in a Greater Position, the reason they couldn't Grasp the Possibilities, was all because they had a Grasshopper Personality. Did you catch what they said about how they saw themselves against the inhabitants in the land of Canaan? "There we saw the giants(the descendants of Anak came from the giants); and we were like grasshoppers in our own sight, and so we were in their sight." The folks down in Canaan, according to Rahab, saw them for who they were, "God's Folks," but they saw themselves as one of the lowest forms of life on the face of the earth. They thought so little of themselves that it caused some to them to lose what was theirs and their children to wait for forty years to reap a blessing. How many times in life have we done this to ourselves? Or better yet, how many of us have this Grasshopper Personality now? Paul writes to the folks down in Rome and asks some of the most powerful questions that a child of God could ever be asked, and then he concludes these questions with and even more powerful answer. In Romans 8 : 31 - 37, we find these questions: What shall we then say to these things? If God be for us, who can be against us? He that spared not his own Son, but delivered him up for us all, how shall he not with him also freely give us all things? Who shall lay anything to the charge of God's elect? It is God that Justifieth. Who is he that condemneth? It is Christ that died, yea rather, that is risen again, who is even at the right hand of God, who also maketh intercession for us. Who shall separate us from the love of Christ? Shall tribulation, or distress, or persecution, or famine, or nakedness, or peril, or sword? As it is written, for thy sake we are killed all the day long; we are accounted as sheep for the slaughter. Answer: Nay, in all these things we are more than conquerors through him that loved us. The word conqueror comes from the Greek word hupernikao (Pronounced, hoop-er-nik-ah'- o) and it means to vanquish beyond, or to gain a decisive victory, but he says that our abilities to conquer goes to a greater extent. We are more than conquerors. Paul basically says here that there is nothing too hard for God to work out in our favor and since we belong to Him we must put away the mind set that causes us to think so little of ourselves. We have to get rid of our Grasshopper Personality.

The point is this, just as God's Folks then, so many of God's Folks now are guilty of theses same things. Some of us could have been in some much better situations years ago, but we failed to recognize that we belong to God, we're God's Property. Some of us could have by now been in better financial situation years ago, but we failed to see that Greater Position. Some of us could have been happier, healthier, living a life full of peace and joy years ago, but we failed to realize what we have in Jesus. The reason why some of us have been, and the reason why some of us are now so defeated in this life, is because we failed to Grasp the Possibilities of what it means to belong to God and where we could be in life seeing that we do belong to the Father of Life. We will never do better until we abandon the low self-esteem of thinking. We have to make Phil. 4:13 (I can do all things, through Christ, which strengthens me) become more than just words.

John so powerfully writes and says in I John 3 : 22, "And whatsoever we ask, we receive of him, because we keep his commandments, and do those things that are pleasing in his sight." I am spiritually convinced that Christians should look like Christians. There's an old saying that suggested that "some of us are so heavenly minded, that we're no earthly good." All this is saying is that before we can get to heaven, there's some things we have to handle down here. Also some of us are so worried about messing up that we are afraid to move up. The idea here is that it's amazing how the people that belong to the creator of the universe can live life in constant defeat. If I could ask a question here: I would like to know is there an idea amongst some of us in the kingdom, thinking that there are certain persons in the kingdom, that should have a life with only little happiness, only a little joy, only a little money, or is it possible for everyone in the kingdom of God to achieve a prosperous life? Now I am fully aware of the fact that prosperity doesn't always mean lots of money, but I refuse to believe that a Christian who is faithfully committed to the cause of Christ will have to always struggle to make ends meet. We must at least be able to envision that God's

Folks can enter into a status, to where we are able to have just as much as he or she needs and desires. The earlier question was asked, because some have made the claim that everybody isn't supposed to be rich, and I would agree to an extent, but I strongly believe that everybody that belongs to the God of heaven, everyone who has confessed faith in Jesus to be the son of God, everyone who has been washed by the blood of the lamb and filled with the Holy Spirit, is able to have a prosperous life, whether it be Faith, Finances, Family or Fitness.

The intentions of these writings are to convince blood washed believers that life here on earth is what we make it to be. Moses told Israel in Deut. 11: 26 - 28, Behold, I set before you this day a blessing and a curse; A blessing, if ye obey the commandments of the Lord your God, which I command you this day: And a curse, if ye will not obey the commandments of the Lord your God, but turn aside out the way which I command you this day, to go after other gods which ye have not known. I reflect back to I John 3 : 22, to help me with the belief that if I please God, then God will please me with the blessings of life. In these writings we will explore the underlining principles that God has shown through His word, telling us, His children, how to live a prosperous life, whether it be Faith, Finances, Family or Fitness.

CHAPTER ONE

Position of Power

CHECK OUT YOUR POSITION

(I Peter 2: 9 - 10) But ye are a chosen generation, a royal priesthood, an holy nation, a peculiar people; that ye should shew forth the praises of him who hath called you out of darkness into his marvelous light; Which in time past were not a people, but are now the people of God; which had not obtained mercy, but now have obtained mercy.

EVERY PERSON WHO HAS BEEN set free by Jesus has been emphatically placed, by God, into a Position of Power. And while we coexist in a world with the children of darkness, it's pivotal that all believers realize and recognize the beauty of this position and the amazing grace that gave us the ability and access to enter into this position. Success for some, is measured by how far they have made it in life. While for others, success is measured by whom they have become. In essences, when you weigh all the accomplishments that one could achieve, none of them would matter when life has expired, unless one had been born again in this life before they leave this life. We that have confessed our faith in Jesus must put an end to the "beat downs" that we give ourselves, by coming into a full understanding of the position we have been allowed to enter into. Now with your spiritual mentality switched to on, check out your position:

CHOSEN GENERATION

Peter says in the above text that "Ye"(All who have been washed in the blood of the lamb) are a chosen generation. Another translation says that "You are an elect race." The Greek term that is used here is the word *eklektos*. According to *Vines Expository Dictionary* the following reference is given:

— *Believers were "chosen" "before the foundation of the world"(cp. "before times eternal," 2 Tim. 1:9), in Christ, Eph. 1:4, to adoption, Eph.1:5; good works, Eph. 2:10; conformity to Christ, Rom. 8:29; salvation from the delusions of the Antichrist and the doom of the deluded, 2 Thess. 2:13; eternal glory, Rom. 9:23.*
— *The source of their "election" is God's grace, not human will, Eph. 1:4,5; Rom. 9:11; 11:5. They are given by God the Father to Christ as the fruit of His death, all being foreknown and foreseen by God, John 17:6; Rom. 8: 29. While Christ's death was sufficient for all men, and is effective in the case of the "elect," yet men are treated as responsible, being capable of the will and power to choose. For the rendering "being chosen as firstfruits,"*

Now despite the Calvinistic theory(T.U.L.I.P.) that certain individuals are chosen from birth, this text refers to what I call a position that God has chosen for man to get into. James Coffman says in his commentary of the New Testament concerning this text that, "this means that God has predestined and appointed all who shall be found IN Christ to eternal glory; but people come under the benefits of such appointments only when they are baptized into Christ and are FOUND IN HIM at the last" (Revelations 14:13). In order for one to be known as the chosen or elect of God they must get into position. Try this for your understanding, lets say a plane is headed from Memphis to New York City, and there are no planned stops on this flight. Now if you know anything about the airports, all of their flights are already planned before you buy your ticket. In other words the airport does not set up a commercial flight just because you buy a ticket. The ticket that you purchase is for a flight that is already headed in the direction you want to go. Now, not only is it already headed in that direction, but regardless if you get on the plane or not it's headed that way. Now if you get on the plane that's headed to New York City, you will reach your destination. The only way you don't reach it, is if you for some reason get off. This position that God has chosen is headed for glory and when a person accepts the terms and enters into the covenant of agreement with God, then that person becomes part of the chosen generation and they will end up in glory, if they stay on board.

ROYAL PRIESTHOOD

Under the Mosaic system only priest had bureau to offer up sacrifices to God for the sins of the people, but the passion on Calvary made it possible for those who have been washed in the blood of the Lamb to be able to offer up his or her own sacrifice(Hebrews 9; 13:15). Since we have been translated into the Lord's Kingdom(Col. 1:13), we are considered as royalty. All of this within itself constitutes us as a royal priesthood.

HOLY NATION

The word Holy here comes from the Greek *hagios*. According to **Vines Expository Dictionary** the following reference is given:

— *This sainthood is not an attainment, it is a state into which God in grace calls men; yet believers are called to sanctify themselves(consistently with their calling, 2 Tim. 1:9), cleansing themselves from all defilement, forsaking sin, living a "holy" manner of life, 1 Peter 1:15; 2 Peter 3:11, and experiencing fellowship with God in His holiness. The saints are thus figuratively spoken of as "a holy temple," 1 Cor. 3:17(a local church); Eph. 2:21(the whole Church), cp. Eph. 5:27; "a holy priesthood," 1 Peter 2:5; "a holy nation," 1 Peter 2:9.*

— *"It is evident that hagios and its kindred words... express something more and higher than hieros(sacred), outwardly associated with God;... something more than semnos(worthy, honorable); something more than hagnos(pure, free from defilement). Hagios is ... more comprehensive ... **it is characteristically godlikeness.***

Notice the last statement of Vine's definition. This brings us to the understanding that this position holds a divine quality. Which helps to understand Peter's assessment in II Peter 1:4 saying that we are *"partakers of the divine nature."* In essence we have obtained a nature that is eccentric(*strange*) to the world, un-vision-able to the eyes of the unspiritual, yet placing us in a category as godly. This nature contrast our old nature Eph. 2: 1 - 8.

A PECULIAR PEOPLE

In the New King James' translation of the Bible this portion is read as "His own special people," which generates a better understanding of how precious this position is to God. The word *Peculiar* is better used as possession in most translations from the Greek word *peripoiesis*. According to **Vines Expository Dictionary** the following reference is given:

—   *"An obtaining, an inquisition," is translated "(God's own) possession" in Eph. 1:14, RV, which may mean "acquisition," AV, "purchased possession;" 1 Pet. 2:9, RV, "God's own possession," AV, "a peculiar (people)."*

Now this is the sum of this matter. The position that we have obtained as blood washed, believers were elected or chosen by God before the foundation of the world. We have the ability to offer spiritual sacrifices to God ourselves, seeing that we are royalty. We have a godlike, divine nature that elevates us to be in a semblance of gods. All while being the Creator of Life's own special possessions. What a dynamic position! Also do not forget that this position is a position of power, which God has put within the believer so "that ye should shew forth the praises of him who hath called you out of darkness into his marvelous light";. In chapter 2 this power that believers possess will be given more attention, as for now let's continue to focus on how phenomenal the position is. Hence the reason why we should take more pride in being a child of the most High God.

CHECK OUT YOUR CONDITION BEFORE YOUR POSITION

Before we move any further in the observance of the grandeur or greatness of this position, we should take a look at the condition we were in before we got into this position. Because when you really understand the magnitude of being pulled out of darkness, you then come to a full awareness of the grace that was given to us through Jesus. Peter says in *I Peter 2 :10, "Which in time past were not a people," "which had not obtained mercy."* Paul says in *Eph. 2:12, "That at that time ye were without Christ, be aliens from the commonwealth of Israel, and strangers from the covenant of promise, having no hope, and without God in the world":. Eph. 2 :1b - 2, "who were dead in trespasses and sins; 2. Wherein in time past ye walked according to the course of this world, according to the prince of the power of the air, the spirit that now worketh in the children of disobedience":*

Your Condition was this:

- *Not a People.*
- *No Mercy.*
- *Aliens from the commonwealth of Israel.*

- *Stranger.*
- *No hope.*
- *Without God.*
- *Walked according to the course of the world.*
- *You served the prince of power of the air(devil).*
- *You were in darkness.*
- *You were dead.*

This is the sum of your condition before your position. You were hopeless and doomed. But God being full of mercy and grace allowed Jesus to strip himself of the heavenly resplendency(glory), come to this wretched earth, took away the wretchedness from those who believe and have now made us his people, given us mercy, made us to be fellow citizens with believing Jews. He now knows us(II Tim. 2: 9). He has raised us from the dead, so that we can walk in the light(I John 1 :7). What a dynamic position. Now watch the dynamics of that transition from darkness to light. We needed grace, so that we could obtain mercy. (An old preacher once said that, Grace is something we needed but didn't deserve, while Mercy is something we needed to keep us from getting what we do deserve.) God brought us from that deadly condition and put us in this lively position.

ALLOW YOURSELF TO SEE YOUR VICTORY

Now here's the big question, if this position is that awesome, then why are so many of the ones that have obtained this position, living so far beneath their potential(ability to succeed in the future)? Why are we so easily defeated by life's blows? One of the devil's greatest weapons against the people of God, is to persuade us to not allow ourselves to see our victories. Remember Israel? When you are not able to see what, God has already done in your life, then it becomes difficult to see God's ability to bring you out of something else. All of us have been through storms that seemed as if they were powered by greater storms, but we're still here. We have lost love ones that we didn't think that we could live without, but we're still here. Some of us were diagnosed with cancer ten years ago, but we're still here. So what happens when we are still troubled by the next issue or issues that come in our life, is that we are not allowing ourselves to see our victories. Remember you are "more than a conqueror". What we must realize is that God has to allow battles to come into our lives, in order to teach us how to fight this good fight of faith. The reason God has us claiming the rough side of the mountain is because if we went up on the smooth side, the only thing that would happen is that we would slide back down. So every rock, every valley, every deep and dark place that we face in our climb helps us reach the top. Until we allow ourselves to see our victories that we have, until we allow ourselves to see the benefits of belonging to God, until we allow ourselves to see the purpose behind the problem, then defeat is not an option, it's a guarantee.

As was stated in the introduction of these writings, let's examine the power of Paul's works in Romans chapter 8 as he lays down the frame work of the victory we have in this position. First of all verse 28, Paul emphatically tells believers that everything that happens in our lives, whether good or bad, it always works in the favor of the people of God(more on purpose in chapter 3). The potency of this position is further shown in the following verses. Verse 29 thru 30, shows us our predestination and out justification and our glorification from being transformed into the image of Jesus. Verse 30 ponders into the mystery of why would a child of God be concerned with the thoughts, ideas, and saying about us by folks on the outside of God. He shows here the sincerity of God's care for his folks. If God is for you why are you worried about the "who" is against you. If God is for you, why are you worried about the needs of this life. We have a problem in our mist, and the problem is not that *we don't have what we need, but the problem is that we don't see what we have.* Paul says that if God spared not His own Son, but delivered him up for us **ALL**, how shall he not, with Him also **FREELY GIVE US ALL THINGS?**

We must understand that if God says all, that means that he leaves nothing out. Which brings about another issue, in the matter of some of God's folks living beneath their potential(ability to succeed in the future)? God has it to give, but it seem that some in the Kingdom don't believe God enough to get. Jesus said in Matthew 6 : 25 - 33:

"*Therefore I say unto you, Take no thought for your life, what ye shall eat, or what ye shall drink; nor yet for your body, what ye shall put on. Is not the life more than meat, and the body than raiment? Behold the fowls of the air: for they sow not, neither do they reap, nor gather into barns; yet your heavenly Father feedeth them. Are ye not much better than they? Which of you by taking thought can add one cubit unto his statue? And why take ye thought for raiment? Consider the lilies of the field, how they grow; they toil not, neither do they spin: And yet I say unto you, that even Solomon in all his glory was not arrayed like one of these. Wherefore, if God so clothe the grass of the field, which today is and tomorrow is cast into the oven, shall he not much more clothe you, O ye of little faith? Therefore take no thought, saying, What shall we eat? What shall we drink? Wherewithal shall we be clothe? (For after all these things do the Gentiles seek:) for your heavenly Father knoweth that ye have need of all things. But seek ye first the kingdom of God, and his righteousness; and* **all these things shall be added unto you.**"

If one does not allow themselves to see the victory given us by God, then one would not comprehend the need to seek the kingdom of God first, to have all these things(necessities of life) added to their life. Just as Israel didn't believe that they could have what God had promised because of what they saw, or better yet what they didn't allow themselves to see, neither will we receive the fullness of what God can do in our lives. To many kingdom children end up focusing on their circumstantial situations to truly see that God is for us and the potential we have through Christ to excel in whatever area of life we choose. Surely none of us want to go through "forty years of wondering" before we finally discover what God has for his folks.

THE POWER OF SEEING YOUR VICTORY

Now watch what Paul tells the folks in Ephesus concerning the ability of seeing our unlimited potential and unlimited victory we have in Jesus:

(Eph. 1 : 18 - 19), " The **eyes of your understanding** being enlightened; that ye may know what is the hope of his calling, and what the riches of the glory of his inheritance in the saints, and what is the exceeding greatness of his power to us-ward who believe, according to the working of his mighty power." Notice the phrase **"eyes of your understanding."** Another translation says, **"eye of your**

heart. The word "understanding" comes from the Greek word *dianoia*, which gives reference to the deep thoughts of the mind(which is the spiritual heart as referred to in scripture). The heart(which is the mind) is the innermost control center of man. It is the seat of understanding, the generator of thoughts, emotions, actions, desires, and words. It is the powering motivation of human life. What is in the heart(mind), will drive the conduct. Paul is saying that the love that God has for us has to become so real to us that we can fully visualize His ability to bless us. When the hope of his calling and the riches of the glory of his inheritance in the saints becomes a reality in our hearts(mind), then our manner of life will change, and every dependency of life is driven by this reality. Then the knowledge of the ability of God will lead you into a lifestyle of comfort and peace that will settle your heart(mind) in the midst of your storms. The eyes of the heart, once they are spiritually opened, can enable one to look out on the world and determine what kind of life one is going to live(potential). When one is spiritually enlightened, he or she knows that God views His children so precious that He would not waste what He paid for(I Cor 6: 19 - 20). Not only would He not waste what He paid for, but He'll most certainly take care of us. However, the beginning condition is that we must allow ourselves to see the love that God has for us and what He is able to do for us.

Now here in lies the unfolding meaning of why the New Testament writers focused so heavily on the knowledge of Christ. Once these spiritual eyes are opened, then a lifestyle of seeking closeness with God becomes ever so common. Which then leads us to a place where we forget about what we see or even have seen and look to what could be.

Everything that was, is now spiritually forgotten(spiritual amnesia). All the bad decisions of your past. All the bad relationships of your past. All the bad experiences of your past are no longer a factor in your life, because now you have a goal that must be reached. Hear the words of Paul as he speaks about himself, when his spiritual eyes became open, when he allowed himself to see the victory he had obtain in Jesus, and when he allowed himself to let go of his past.(Phil 3:8 - 14) *"Yet indeed I also count all things loss for the excellence of the knowledge of Christ Jesus my Lord, for whom I have suffered the loss of all things, and count them as rubbish and be found in Him. . . . .that I may know Him and the power of His resurrection, and the fellowship of His sufferings, being conformed to His death, if, by any means, I may attain to the resurrection from the dead. . . .I do not count myself to have apprehended; but one thing I do, forgetting those things which are behind and reaching forward to those things which are ahead, I press toward the goal for the prize of the upward call of God in Christ Jesus."* God's folks have to allow themselves to see the victory that we have in Jesus_

RELATIONSHIP ENHANCEMENT LEADS TO SPIRITUAL ADVANCEMENT

So since this position of being a child of God is so blessed and we have to allow ourselves to see the blessedness of it, by allowing the Spirit to open the spiritual eyes of our hearts(mind). The question now becomes: How do I tap into the deepness of understanding the potency of being one of God's elect? In other words, how can one get a full assurance implanted in their heart to know that God is really able to bless us, build us up, and bring to pass the desires of our hearts? Better yet, how do I reach that level to where I can receive whatsoever I ask for(I John 3:22)? How do I reach that level of spiritual maturity to where I can love my enemy, and be able to sustain myself if I'm struck on the right cheek(Matt. 5: 38 - 48)? How do I reach that level of getting closer to God so that I can have the same mind as Christ, just as God has commanded me to have(Phil. 2 : 5)? How do I open the spiritual eyes of my understanding so that I may be able to look not one the now and see the after? The key to all of this and more is that we must enhance out relationship with God so that we can spiritually advance toward God.

How many times have we heard people say, "I know the Lord?" Now to be honest, the issue is not whether you know the Lord, but the issue is, "Does the Lord know you"(II Tim. 2 : 19). For example, I know exactly who Bill Gates is, but Bill Gates doesn't know me, if you can get that. If Bill Gates were to say that he's going to give everyone he knows a million dollars, it would not benefit me because I know him, seeing that he doesn't know me. Other children in this world know who I am, but the only children I am obligated to take care of are my own. The reality is this, the children that are in the home of their father will reap all the benefits of the father because of the closeness of that relationship. In the story of the prodigal son, the son that stayed at home had to be reminded by his father that everything the father has and has ever had, belongs also to him because he has always been there with his father. It is important that we understand that if we are going to reach this level of spiritual knowledge and understanding, we must engage ourselves into some vital spiritual exercise. We have got to get to **"Know God"** and **"Allow God to Know Us."**

The word *know*, that is often used in scripture, occasionally is from the Greek word *ginosko* and the word frequently indicates a relationship between the person "knowing" and the object known. So in this respect, what is "known" is of value or importance to the one who knows, and hence the establishment of the relationship. To broaden your understanding of what is being said, this refers especially of God's knowledge of his children that are diligently seeking him(Hebrews 11:6). Paul says in I Cor. 8:3, "if any man love God, the same is known of Him. In Gal 4:9, Paul shows here the "knowing" suggests approval and bears the meaning "to be approved." The same thought of appreciation as well as "knowledge" underlies several statements concerning the "knowledge" of God and His truth on the part of believers,(John 8:32; 14:20, 31; 17:3; Gal. 4:9 (1ˢᵗ part); 1 John 2:3, 13, 14; 4:6,8,16; 5:20). In simpler terms this word refer to a intimate and productive relationship. In Genesis 4 : 1, the scriptures say, "And Adam *knew* his wife; and she conceived, and bare Cain." In this knowledge of really knowing who God is and most of all having God know you, something will be produced from this relationship. The product of this relationship will be spiritual advancement. Because of the time spent in the enhancement of this relationship with God, we will advance to that level of complete understanding of why trouble gets in our way and why we are put down when we're trying to do good. We develop a mind set that allows us to love the unlovable, to have joy in monstrous circumstances. We learn how to trust God in every aspect, in every phase, and in every manner of this life. Once you reach, this level then life gets better. Once you reach this level in this relationship with God, then you have something to look forward to besides the substances of this life(Phil. 1 : 21 -23). Even when those who are close to you leave you, for whatever reason, this relationship will keep you in comfort.

In essence the fabric of this relationship is woven from the wheel of repetitive examination of the oracles of God. In other words *we got to look in the book(Bible)*. We have got to spend time in the word of God so that we become familiar with our Father's commands. Moreover, we have to become familiar with God's word so that we can find God's purpose for our life. Truth be told, we don't know enough to help ourselves, so God gives us what we need to advance ourselves toward a closer relationship with Him. Somebody said once the that the Bible stands for "*Basic Instructions Before Leaving Earth.*" All of us must one day leave this place and none of us knows the way and unless we allow God to show us, then where He is, we can not go. Peter said in I Peter 2 : 1 - 3. "*Wherefore laying aside all malice, and all guile, and hypocrisies, and envies, and all evil speaking, as newborn babes, desire the sincere milk of the word, that ye may grow thereby: if so be ye have tasted that the Lord is gracious.*" All of us who have confessed our faith in Christ have certainly tasted the graciousness of God, and the reason why God has allowed us to taste his goodness is so that we can learn to trust in Him and from that trust, a production of blessings will spill over into our life(II Cor 9:8; Mal 3:10). Which helps us to understand why the Psalmist said in Ps 34: 8," *O Taste and see that the Lord is good:* **blessed is the man that trusted in him.**" We are fortunate and well off when we learn to trust our Father. We are fortunate and well off, by being positioned as the peoples(folks) of God.

If we were to take a closer look at each of the epistles written by Paul, we would see a heavy revolve around studying the scriptures. For example notice the things that Paul tells Timothy, a young preacher in the 1st century who possibly had one of the spiritual gifts mentioned in I Cor. 12(see also I Tim. 4:14; II Tim. 1 : 6). He tells him in I Timothy 4 :13, *"Till I come, give attendance to reading, to exhortation, to doctrine."* He then tells in verses 15 - 16 *"Meditate upon these things; give thyself wholly to them; that they profiting may appear to all. Take heed unto thyself, and unto the doctrine; continue in them: for in doing this thou shalt both save yourself, and them that hear thee."* Also notice what Paul says in the later part of verse 15, "that thy profiting may appear to all." When your relationship with God advances, there will undoubtably be visible evidence that God is working in you and for you. Everybody you come in contact with will see just what God has done for you and to you and through you. Paul even goes a little further in II Timothy 2 : 15 - 19. He says "Study to show thyself approved unto God, a workman that needs not to be ashamed, rightly dividing the word of truth." Now watch what happens from the examination or the studying of God's word in verse 19a, "Nevertheless the foundation of God stands sure, having this seal, *The Lord knows them that are his."* So as it has been already stated, the issue is not whether you know the Lord, but the issue is does the Lord know you. Simply put, relationship enhancement leads to spiritual advancement. When Paul wrote to the churches in Galatia, to debate the Judaizing teachers, he asked the Galatians a remarkable question in Gal. 4:8 -9, *"Howbeit then, when ye knew not God, ye did service unto them which by nature are no gods. But now, after that ye*

have known God, or rather are known of God, *how turn ye again to the weak and beggarly elements, whereunto ye desire again to be in bondage?"* If we consider the validity of this question that Paul asks to the 1ˢᵗ century saints in Galatia, it could very easily transcend down the corridors of time to us today. It's not spiritually logical for a child of God to have come into this enhanced relationship with God to turn and go back to their weak and beggarly(cheap) old self(Hebrews 6: 4-6); especially , if he or she has been engaged in the spiritual advancement process. Paul tells those in Colosse 3: 9 - 10, *"Do not lie to one another, since you have put off the old man with his deeds, and have put on the new man who is **renewed in knowledge** according to the image of Him who created him."* Just as constant exercise helps the physical body become stronger, so must constant spiritual exercise be done in order for God's folks to reach that enhanced relationship. Then you'll be able to see the beauty of this position of being a child of God. You'll be able to handle the struggles of this life. You'll be able to live the life a child of God should live, while here on this earth. Simply because this is an awesome position being one of God"Folks". Jesus said in John 14:23, "if a man love me, he will keep my word: and my Father will love him, and we will come unto him, and make our abode with him."

CHAPTER TWO

Power To Accomplish A Purpose

John 1 : 11 - 12, "He came unto his own, and his own received him not. But as many as received him, to them gave he power to become the sons of God, even to them that believe on his name."

Eph. 3 : 20, "Now unto him that is able to do exceeding abundantly above all that we ask or think, according to the power that works in us,."

Once the blessedness of our position has become reality within our hearts, then we must also understand the ability acquired by entering into this position. There is power associated with the life of all believers. Everyone who has named the name of Jesus and who have been washed in the blood of the lamb, has power. Those whom God has adopted into His heavenly and earthy family has been given *"Power to Accomplish A Purpose."* By this being so, it becomes more a wonder to see so many of God's

Folks living beneath their potential(ability to succeed in the future). We have power to help direct the outcome of our lives and our future and the future of our families. We have the power to bring ourselves out of horrible pits. We have the power to destroy depression. We can destroy defeating principalities and deepening debt. We have the power to get over merciless moments, abusive affairs, sorrowful situations, and critical circumstances. God has place within all of His children the ability to gain the victory.

God's folks have the ability to do things that unbelievers in the world can't do(Phil. 4 : 13). We have the ability to see things that the unbelievers in the world can't see(Eph. 1 :18). We can comprehend the uncomprehensible, we can achieve that which seems difficult. We can attain that which seems to be unattainable. We have this power simply because we serve a God who is able to resurrect the dead and calls those things which do not exist as though they did(Romans 4 : 17). The Hebrew writer records in his writing in Hebrews 13 : 8 that Jesus Christ is the same today, as He was yesterday, and He'll be the same forever as He is today. God said through Malachi in Mal. 3 : 6, "For I am the Lord, I change not." Since the Lord does not change, then we should have comfort to know that if God took care of our brothers and sisters whom we read about in scripture He will take care of us now. If God restored Job's faith, fitness, family, and finances surely He can do the same for you. Since you have power, stop saying what you can't do.

POWER TO REFRESH AND REFORM

While instructing the young preacher Timothy, Paul in II Tim. 2 : 6 -7 tells him,   *"Therefore I remind you to stir up the gift of God which is in you through the laying on of my hands. For God has not given us a spirit of fear, but of power and of love and of a sound mind."*

Here was a young man who possibly had a very timid nature and he needed to know that he was able to do the work, that God had sent him there to do in Ephesus. Paul tells Timothy to remember or refresh his thinking on what he has in him. With Timothy knowing and understanding what was in him, then he could know that he had the ability to reform or change things for the better. In the process of Paul refreshing Timothy's mind, he directs Timothy's heart toward what God has given him, showing him what he, through God, was able to do. Notice the word *power* in 2 Tim. 1:7, it comes from the Greek word *dunamis*. This word gives reference to having a mighty ability or strength. It brings forth an idea of one having the ability to perform miracles. It's the same word that Jesus would use in Acts 1:8, concerning what the Apostles would receive from the Holy Spirit. This power that the Apostles received gave them the ability to reshape, to reform and change that which seemed unchangeable(Acts 3:1 - 11). Now Paul uses this same word to help Timothy understand what God has given to him. With the young preacher understanding that he has this kind of power to reform outcomes and situations, he would be lead to not be afraid of stepping out on faith and doing what it took to make his life and his circumstances a little easier. It would help him properly lead this church. Now, I want you to understand that Timothy may not have had the ability to make a lame man walk or a blind man to see physically. However, he did have the ability to do it spiritually. He may not have had the ability to restore a thing he had lost,

21

but spiritually he had the ability to control what he would find(Matt. 7 : 7, "ask and you will receive, seek and you will find, knock and the door will be opened"). In essence, the power that Timothy had is the same power that God has given each of his children. So when we are afraid to step out and try something different, when we are afraid to seek better conditions, we accept defeat and basically *"spit in the eyes of our potential."* When we accept low standards, we enter into a low standard acceptance stage, in which we have nothing better to look forward to. We have then, allowed the devil to fool us into thinking that nothing good can happen. However, those whom God has redeemed from darkness, have the power to make their lives better(potential). God's folks have the power to look into the eye of a storm and see the greatness that's on the other side of that storm.

Now if your wondering how can this author assume that we, God's folks, have the ability or power to reform our lives, then we'll take a deeper look into this power that God's Folks have. The Greek word **dunamis** unfolds into our English word "dynamite." Now, when dynamite is ignited it causes a complete change to whatever it comes in contact with. It reshapes a thing to make it look different. When dynamite does its job, it becomes obvious that alterations have been made. Paul also used this word to describe what the Gospel was able to do. Romans 1 : 16, *"For I am not ashamed of the gospel of Christ: for it is the power(dunamis) of God unto salvation to every one that believes; to the Jew first, and also to the Greek."* The Gospel has the ability to change whomever it comes in contact with and the change is very obvious. This is what makes Paul's words to Timothy shine with such brightness. Here we are told that God has given us the ability to reform our own lives, and if that isn't enough to convince us of what we have in us, Paul takes it a little further in Eph. 3 :20. Paul says there *"Now unto Him that is able to do exceeding abundantly above all that we ask or think, according to the Power(dunamis) that works in us,."* Now watch this awesome fact, Paul says in I Corinthians 10 : 25, 28 that God owns everything. Now get this, the God that is responsible for the existence of everything is able to do anything base off of what He has put in you. As powerful as dynamite is, it can do nothing until it is ignited. Therefore that spiritual dynamite that God has put in you is ready and waiting for you to ignite and change your circumstance. God can do more than we need Him to do. He can give us more than what we can ask for, and if that weren't enough, Paul even points to the fact that we aren't even capacitated enough mentally to think of the fullness of His ability to work in us and for us. What makes this fact so dazzling is that Paul tells us that these abilities, which are of God, are activated through us. How awesome is it to know that God has put in us what we need to get what we want out of Him. So if you have been struggling in your life, this author has some questions for you: Where are you now? How did you get there? Why are you still there? How long are you going to stay there? Now if where you are now, is a dark place in life, ignite your power(dunamis, dynamite) and get out. If you have been there for years on top of years, ignite your power and tell yourself that its been long enough. If the reason you have been there is because of you or someone else, ignite your power and forgive them and especially forgive yourself and move on. If you have had no idea of how long you where going to safe in that dark place, ignite your power and decide that today it's over. Set ablaze your potential(ability to succeed in the future) today.

Even if the you have allowed the devil to make you think that you are nothing, God is able to perform an *"exnihilo"* and what that means is that He is able to take nothing and turn it into something. So seeing that we serve a God who is able to turn nothing into something and He has given us the power to refresh and reform our conditions, you need to understand that your finances can change, you family can change, your fitness can change, and most importantly your faith can change. One of the very reasons why others outside of God should be attracted to God is by what they see in us. We have the power to accomplish a purpose and I believe that we have an ultimate purpose to show the world God in us(Matthew 5 : 14 - 16). I believe that when we live in our purpose and use our power to change our lives, then the world will notice and want to be where we are and have what we have. How can anybody want to become a Christian if they see Christians struggling with life, never being happy, living without joy, and even continuously being in financial ruin? I believe that Acts 2:47 is a direct result of Acts 2 :44 - 46. Seeing that the saints lived the way they were living and behaving the way they were behaving, loving the way they were loving one another, those on the outside looking in wanted to get in , on what they saw God doing for his folks and what they saw God folks doing for one another. God's Folks are called lights for a reason, not just because we need a light to find our way through darkness, but so that others can find their way out of darkness. We are God's lighthouses, set on a hill, guiding the lost ships of men through darkness. Therefore, we need not to let another day pass by without us understanding that we have the power to refresh and reform our lives with the help of God. David said this way in Ps 34 : 17 -19, *"The righteous cry, and the Lord hears and delivers them out of all their troubles. The Lord is near to them that are of a broken heart; and saves such as be of a contrite(sorrowful) spirit. Many are the afflictions of the righteous; but the Lord delivers him out of them all."*

BE THE CAUSE OF YOUR BLESSING

John 1 : 11 - 12, "He came unto his own, and his own received him not. But as many as received him, to them gave he power to become the sons of God, even to them that believe on his name."

Remember, when you were younger and your parents told you that if you got good grades or if you did your chores you would get an allowance? Now, the only way you didn't get your allowance was if you did not do what you were told to do. On the other hand when you did what you were told, you automatically placed yourself in position to get what was promised. You had a right to that allowance, not just because of what you did, but also because who it was that made you the promise of the allowance. On your job, you have a right to receive wages at the end of the work week, not just because you did the work, but also because you are part of that company. We have a right to be blessed, simply because of whom we belong to and we have been allowed, by blood, to be able to do what it takes to cause a blessing to come into our lives. The reason why you got that allowance was because you caused it by what you did and as long as you stayed there in the house with your parents you were entitled to everything that your parents were able to do for you. As long as you stay on your job, you are entitled to everything your company is able to do for you. As long as we stay on God's side, we are entitled to everything that God is able to do for his children.

The word Power in John 1 :12 is from the Greek word *exousia* and it means "to have the right or privilege." To be privileged means that you are favored by God. Once you accepted the call of God, and enter into the election of a saint, you are favored by God(*Proverbs 3:1 - 4, "My son, do not forget my law, but let your heart keep my commands; for length of days and long life and peace they will add to you. Let not mercy and truth forsake you; Bind them around you neck, write them on the tablet of your heart, and so find favor and high esteem in the sight of God and man.*) This favor entitles the "Folks" of God to reap the benefits of being His children. Whenever someone has the right or privilege to anything that has value, they without a doubt would want what they have a right to, even if they feel that a struggle is needed to obtain what is rightfully theirs. Now here's where the problem comes in for many in the Kingdom, we don't put up enough of a fight for what should be ours. Now don't get confused, sometimes you do have to fight for what is yours, remember the Civil Rights Movement. Blacks had to fight for what was theirs, without violence but with words and marching. When Israel, finally crossed over Jordan, there where people in the land that God had given to them. To get what was theirs they had to go in and fight. In Genesis 32: 24 - 32, we read of Jacob wrestling with a man who is thought to be an angel. In verse 26, the man tells Jacob to "let me go, for the day breaks," but Jacob's answer was, "I will not let you go, except you bless me." Jacob somehow knew that this man

whom he had come in contact with had the ability to bless
him and he wrestled all night until he got what he thought
he had a right too. Now watch the spiritual application of
this event as it applies to you. Jacob was the "Blessee" the
man(angel, whom Jacob said was God. Gen. 32:30) was
the "Blesser", Jacob knew that the blessings were tied to the
"Blesser" and he was determined to be blessed no matter
how long it took to get the blessing. We struggle with the
idea of knowing that we need God to bless us, but we are
not willing to do what it takes to really get blessed. Now
there are two things that are involved in this process that
requires us to hold on, like Jacob, until we get what we
want. Notice the next two sections:

P. U. S. H.
(PRAY UNTIL SOMETHING HAPPENS)

I use to hear people say, that you should pray for what
you want just one time, then just have enough faith that
you'll get it. Now if you believe that, then that's fine. But
the problem with this view is that some who hold this
thought are saying that if you pray more than one time
for the same thing, then you are showing a lack of faith.
But what does the scripture say? Notice Luke 18 : 1 -8,
*"Then He spoke a parable to them, that men always ought to
pray and not lose heart, saying: "There was in a certain city
a judge who did not fear God nor regard man. Now there
was a widow in that city; and she came to him, saying, 'Get
justice for me from my adversary.' And he would not for a
while; but afterward he said within himself, 'Though I do not
fear God nor regard man, yet because this widow troubles
me I will avenge her, lest by her continual coming she weary
me." Then the Lord said, "Hear what the unjust judge said.*

And shall God not avenge His own elect who cry out day and night to Him, though He bears long with them? I tell you that He will avenge them speedily. Nevertheless, when the Son of Man comes, will He really find faith on the earth?" Here Jesus shows us that we need to *"PUSH,"* pray until something happens. Notice something about this widow in the parable, it wasn't that she troubled the unjust judge because she couldn't find anyone else to help; but, she continued to go to him because she knew that he was the only one who could help. In our new life with God, we have to know that God is the only one who can deliver us out of whatever it is we may get into. We need to know that God is the only one who can give us what we need and what we want, but we have to ask. Jesus said in Matthew 7 : 7 - 11, *"Ask, and it will be given to you; seek and you will find; knock and it will be opened to you. For everyone who asks receives, and he who seeks finds, and to him who knocks it will be opened. Or what man is there among yo who, if his son asks for bread, will give him a stone? Or if he asks for a fish, will he give him a serpent? Or if he asks for a fish, will he give him a serpent? If you then, being evil, know how o give good gifts to your children, how much more will your Father who is in heaven give good thing to those who ask Him_* The older folks used to say, *"A closed mouth won't get feed,"* so whatever we desire to have from the Lord we have got to ask.

Now here's the good part. Not only does Jesus teach us to ask for what we want but he shows us that the more we ask the more faith we exhibit toward our Heavenly Father(Luke 18 : 8). Jesus tells us here that if this unjust judge who has no fear of God, can help this widow, surely the Great Jehovah on High will tend to the cries of his children, if we "PUSH." Jesus in the garden of Gethsemane prayed three times that God would "let this cup pass from me." Paul in II Cor. 12, prayed three times that the Lord would remove a thorn from his flesh. Paul told the folks in Thessalonika in I Thess. 5 : 17 "Pray without ceasing." Paul told the Ephesians in Eph. 6 : 18, "Praying always with all prays and supplication in the Spirit, and watching there unto with all perseverance and supplication for all things." The scriptures are clear, God wants us to depend on Him so much that we come to the understanding that He is the only one who can deliver to us what we need and deliver us from whatever may cause us pain. We must "PUSH."

Now before we leave this portion there is a very important element you need to know. In our pray life, it would help us to understand that we should not "just pray for a blessing", but for "the course to the blessing." Here what I mean, in Psalms 25, David was requesting the favor of God. Now notice the things he asks for in verses 4 and 5. He says, "_Show me Your ways, O Lord; Teach me Your paths. Lead me in Your truth and teach me, for You are the God of my salvation; On You I wait all the day._" David doesn't just pray for the blessing, he prays for the course to the blessing. Notice the course: **Show me Your ways, Teach me Your paths, Lead me in Your truth.** A _course is defined as a direction followed or intended. The way in which something progresses or develops. A procedure adopted to deal with a situation._ The key to this is that without knowing the course to the blessing, it becomes difficult to get back to the blessing. So therefore, in our pray life we need to ask God to help us understand the _way_, the _path_, and the _truth_ so that your life is filled with the knowledge how to deal with multiple situations. Moreover, we need to ask God for the strength to stay on the course and the awareness to know to get back on the course, if you have fallen off. There is an old saying, "Give a man a fish and you feed him for a day, but teach a man how to fish and you feed him for a lifetime." You see, just needing a "quick fix" ought not to be our request to God. What we need are long term solutions. We need to know the course of *financial blessing* and we need the strength to stay on course(II Corinthians. 9 : 6 - 10). We need to know the course of *family blessings* and we need the strength to stay on course(Colossians 3: 18 - 21). We need to know the course of *fitness blessings* and we need the strength to stay on course(I Corinthians 6: 19 - 20). We need to know the course of *faith blessings* and we need the strength to stay on course(Romans 10 : 17). Let us seek God's course which will lead us to God's continual favor.

WORK LIKE IT DEPENDS ON YOU, BELIEVE LIKE IT DEPENDS ON GOD

Once we see the need to *PUSH* and we get on the God's *course*, there is something else we must do. In Matthew 7 : 7, Jesus does not just tell us to ask and wait for God to deliver, but he also says "seek" and "knock." Which means, that after you ask God to do His part you need to get up and do your part. Remember Jacob and his wrestling with a man or angel all night. He asks the man to bless him and while he asked he held on and would not let go and he held on all night until he got blessed. Jacob held on and wrestled because he must have figured that in order to get what he wanted he had to do what he needed to do. Even though he left the wrestling match limping, he got what he was wrestling for. Now here's the power. It wasn't just what he got that blessed him, but whom he became after he was blessed. His name was change to Israel, which is to say a "prince with God." We have to work like it depends on us and believe like it depends on God. Watch what James said in James 2 : 17 - 20, "_Thus also faith by itself, if it does not have works, is dead. But someone will say, "You have faith, and I have works." Show me your faith without your works and I will show you my faith by my works. You believe that there is one God. You do well. Even the demons believe and tremble_ But do you want to know, O foolish man, that faith without works is dead?" Now here's the just of it all. When you have finished praying for the Lord to deliver you out of your financial struggles, you need to get up and look for ways to cut you spending, look for another or better job, look for a way to lessen your wants. Most of the time when we have more month at the end of our money, instead of more money at the end of the month is simply because our wants out weight our needs. Practical examples: Stop buying a $100 worth of groceries and then go out to eat. Stay away from those stores that seem to suck money out of your pockets when you just went in for one thing. Leave those credit cards alone. Save more, so that you will have more and finance less. Get rid of either that house phone or that cell phone, why do we need two phones? We have got to work like it depends on us, and believe like it depends on God.

If your family is going in the wrong direction, don't just pray that God will fix it, get up and do something. Seek counseling for your family, sit down and talk with your husband, wife, or children. Don't lose your family without a fight. One of the most devious ways the devil

31

tries to use to destroy the church is by attacking the family. If he can break down the solid structure of the family then he can begin to break down the church. Notice that one qualification of elders and deacons is that they have their families in order, and if their families are in order, the better influence they can have on leading the church family into order. Don't just pray that your children make the right decisions, help them make the right decisions. Show them the right ways to take. Show them the right attitude to have. Your family is worth the effort. As a believer you have the "Power To Accomplish A Purpose."

CHAPTER THREE

Purpose to Receive the Promise

REMEMBER JOSEPH WHO WAS SOLD by his brothers. Years later they are reunited and his brothers conceived a thought that he would return the evil that they committed to him. Josheph's reply to them shows us the true meaning of *purpose*. *Purpose* is the reason for which something is done or for which something exists. In Genesis 50 : 20, *"Joseph said, "But as for you, you meant evil against me; but God meant it for good, in order to bring it about as it is this day, to save many people alive."* Had God not allowed Joseph to suffer at the hands of his brothers, then the family of Israel would not have been saved from the great famine. Had not Joseph suffered evil by his own family, then the nation of Israel would not have multiplied as they did. As the scriptures unfold down through the corridors of time, we see the purpose behind the evil that was done by Joseph's brothers to bring to pass a marvelous outcome for the people of God. Need I remind you that Judah, was one of the them who were saved by Joseph from the famine. It was from the tribe of Judah, that a man after God's own heart was raised up to reign as King and from his loins came our Savior Jesus.

God has always worked through purpose. It is through purpose that God achieves His awesome work in the lives of believers. It is through purpose that God is able to manifest the appearance of His glory upon His "folks," so that the world may see true light. The Apostle Paul said it best in Romans 8 : 28, "And we know all things work together for good, for them that love God and for them that are the called according to his purpose." Now here is a text that's known by many, even some who are not so familiar with a lot of scripture. Now it must be understood that this text does not necessarily predict triumph over adversity in this life, although it does apply. We have to consider also the fact that this reference is to being delivered from a life of agony into the everlasting abode of the Almighty. Paul says "to live is Christ, but to die is gain"(Phil 1 : 21). In Luke 16, we read of Lazarus and the rich man, and how Lazarus suffers in life and the rich man lived plentifully. They both died and Lazarus was carried into "Abraham's Bosom," which describes the beauty of dying in the Lord and escaping the pains of this life. There is, however, still a place to believe that these words of Paul would apply to the troubles that we face in this life. Showing us that it is true to believe that, "trouble doesn't last always." So with that in mind, notice the spiritual reasoning that is involved in the process of "all things working together for good." Take a look at the articles that are involved: *And we know, Them that love God, Them that are Called, According to his purpose.* Now lets examine each part:

WE KNOW

To get the idea of this portion of this text, a question should be imposed here. How do "We Know?" Paul said in Romans 5 : 3 - 4, "*And not only so, but we glory in tribulations also: knowing(ido) that tribulation works patience; And patience, experience; and experience, hope.*" *Experience* is how "we know." The word "know" comes from the Greek word *ido*, which means "to see." To see things opens the gates of experience. Experience simply means having gone through a thing or things. Experience shows that an individual is familiar with a set of circumstances or directions, seeing that they have been that way before. So the reason why we should know that all things, including difficulties, work together for good is because all of us have seen these things or similar things before. It would also be good to understand that experience should determine the response to the circumstance. In other words, how we respond to the trouble that comes is determined by how much we learned from our past problems that we got over. So Paul could say to the believers in Rome that "we know," and the way that we know is that we have been this way or we have seen these thing before. For example, the reason why you would not touch a pot of boiling water without oven mitts is because something in your past has given you the knowledge that you could be burned. Experience is said to be our best teacher, and I would agree. However, I would take it a little farther and say that, a better teacher is learning from others mistakes. Romans 15 : 4, "*For whatever things were written before were written for our learning, that we through the patience and comfort of the Scriptures might have hope.*" God has given us examples in the scriptures of how difficult life can be when His children fail to trust

35

in Him. The example of Israel in the wilderness, offers us a powerful lesson on what it means to turn to God, to turn from God, and to turn on God, so that we would be less likely to follow the same regretful paths. Paul helps us with this in I Corinthians 10 : 5 - 11, *"But with most of them God was not well pleased, for their bodies we scattered in the wilderness. Now these things became our example, to the intent that we should not lust after evil things as they also lusted. And do not become idolaters as were some of them. As it is written, "The people sat down to eat and drink, and rose up to play." Nor let us commit sexual immorality, as some of them did, and in one day twenty-three thousand fell; nor let us tempt Christ, as some of them also tempted, and were destroyed by serpents; nor complain, as some of them also complained, and were destroyed by the destroyer. Now all these things happened to them as example, and they were written for our admonition, upon whom the ends of the ages have come."* Coupling all these things together, scripture and ones owns activities in life, give us the experience to say, "WE KNOW."

THEM THAT LOVE GOD

Them that love God are those who have developed that understanding of what it means to Love Him. God is love and being that He is love, it stands true that we have to learn what love is. Now one way we learn what the love of God means is by our Heavenly Father allowing us to go through persecution or chastisement(Hebrews 12 : 5 - 11). When we were children and we received a spanking from our parents we didn't really understand why; but now that we are older, we now know that it was because they loved us and wanted us to do what was right.

We understand now that all those spankings and all those "nos," where signs of concern for our well being. So is it also with the Almighty God. When we understand His love for us, then we understand the love we must have toward Him. Jesus defines it this way, "if you love me, you

will keep my commandments..... He that has my commandments and keeps them, he it is that loves me(John 14 : 15, 21)." Christ's apostles stressed the same truth: This is the love of God, that we keep his commandments(1 John 5:3). This is love, that we should walk after his

commandments(2 John 1:6). With logic applied, if there is no love for God, then the chance of all things working together for good is slim to none. So therefore, love for God is needed for God to work in your favor. A willingness to submit to the will of God, would be the evidence that one is in love with the Almighty Jehovah.

THEM THAT ARE CALLED
ACCORDING TO HIS PURPOSE

The word "Called" is from the Greek word _kletos_ which means "invited." Just as we discussed in chapter 1, this does not mean that some have been chosen from birth to be saved. But this shows that invitation that God gives all men through the gospel. Those who are "called" are simply modes of designating the saved. It and the expression "those that love God are descriptive, not of different persons, but of the same persons. Who are the called, and how does the calling occur? Paul's answer was this:

Whereunto(unto salvation) He called you through the gospel, to the obtaining of the glory of our Lord Jesus Christ(II Thess. 2 :14).

In one sense, the entirety of human kind are called by the gospel, as was by Christ's express command that the divine call should be proclaimed to the whole world; but the phrase "according to his purpose" delimits the persons here spoken of to them that fulfilled God's purpose through their conviction or response to the call. *Called according to his purpose* ...means to be called in one body (the church) (Col 3:15) and that through the church there might be made known the manifold wisdom of God, according to the *eternal purpose which he purposed in Christ Jesus our Lord* (Eph 3 : 10 - 11). Paul here did not speak of an individual, but the whole church of the saved. That body(church) is composed of the whole count of the redeemed which is indeed the called and foreordained to everlasting glory; but of an individual person, it must be said that he is called from before all time and predestinated to everlasting life. Only if his affirmative response to God's call has brought him into union with Christ, and if he so abides within the ark of safety called the Church(Eph 5: 23).

With these things now in mind, we can see that those who have learned how to love God by walking by his commandments, and who have been called by the gospel and are doing their best to stay grounded, are entitled to a life blessed by God. Then we can be strong enough to make it through this life and go home to glory. So instead of crying why me, why is this happening to me, why am I suffering this way, we should understand that God has a purpose behind the problem. Just as we want the best for our children, so does God want the best for his folks/ children. Even if it seems that God could have done it another way, just trust His way. For God has spoken to us through Isaiah and said, *"for my thoughts are not your*

38

thoughts, neither are yours ways my ways, saith the Lord. For as the heavens are higher than the earth, so are my ways higher than your ways, and my thoughts than your thoughts (Isa 58 : 8-9).

STRENGTH IS CONCEIVED FROM WEAKNESS

II Cor. 12 : 7 - 9 *"And lest I should be exalted above measure through the abundance of the revelations, there was given to me a thorn in the flesh, the messenger of Satan to buffet me, lest I should be exalted above measure. For this thing I besought the Lord thrice, that it might depart from me. And he said unto me, My grace is sufficient for thee; for my strength is made perfect in weakness. Most gladly therefore will I rather glory in my infirmities, that the power of Christ may rest upon me."*

Notice something about the above text; Paul wanted something removed. God said no. Why did God say no, even though this thing was causing one of His own pain. Why did God say no, even though one of His most dedicated servants was in pain. Well, He said no because no was the right answer to Paul's prayer. Where is the word no in the text you might ask? Well, let's look at it this way, if the answer had been yes, then God would have removed the "thorn in the flesh" as Paul had asked Him to do, not just once, not just twice, but thrice or three times. Sometimes the best answer that God can give us in the mist of our troubles is no. Now before you get confused, remember that "all things(even no) work together for good."

Now why did God allow not only the thorn to stay in the flesh, but why did God allow it to come in the first place? Paul says ""lest I should be exalted above measure through the abundance of the revelations. .. lest I should be exalted above measure." There was a chance that Paul could have begun to think that he was more than what he really was or he could have gotten "beside himself" and forget his true mission. So God allows the "thorn in the flesh" to humble or to keep Paul humble. Sometimes our "Mess is a Message" and the message is the purpose of the mess. God tells us, through our mess, that we need to be humble or we need to be stronger. Notice what Jesus says to Paul in verse 9, "My grace is sufficient for thee: for my strength is made perfect in weakness" The word Sufficient means "enough." In other words, God would have us to know that His grace is enough to get us through the storms of this life. We need to understand this, because a lot of time when we get in our troubles, we sometimes try to get ourselves out by using the world's means instead of God's. Grace is enough_ It was enough to bring us out of darkness and it is enough to get us out of trouble. The song writer knew what he was talking about when he wrote that song and said, *"Amazing grace, how sweet the sound that saved a wretch like me. I once was lost, but now I'm found. Was blind but now I see."* Grace is enough_

Since grace is enough, it compels us to stay within the safety of God arms. It compels us to abide in the ship(Acts 27: 31) and if we so abide, then the weaknesses that we are experiencing in the present are working to build up our spiritual muscles. Remember, how you felt the first time you did some exercises, how sore your muscles were. After some time had passed you continued to perform the exercise again and again, those muscles that you were using, got so strong that it took a little more to hurt you the way it did the first time you worked out. The same applies to our spiritual being. As strange as it may sound, the more you go through, the stronger you'll get, especially if we realize who is behind or who is allowing the pain to come in our lives and who is allowing the pain to stay for a while. The Lord tells us "My strength is made perfect in weakness" then His strength(not our own) leads us to "glory." God has to replace our strength with His strength so that we can "take it, until we make it."

A TRANSFORMED MIND

This is part of the purpose that God has laid out so that we can receive a "greater weight of glory." The word "Purpose" comes from the Greek word *prothesis* which means "a setting forth." God has set everything in motion that will work in the favor of his "folks." The Alpha and the Omega knows everything and just what kind of a "thorn" we need and how long to leave it in us, to propel us into a mind set that is like Christ(Phil. 2:5). Without this mind set we cannot achieve the things that we would like to achieve here on earth. Which then would also prevent us from going home to glory. This is the mind set that the devil does not want us to possess because it destroys his effectiveness. Without this mind set , then our setbacks in life will keep us back. When you have this mind set then you realize that your setbacks are setups for comebacks. Peter says in I Peter 4 : la, *"Forasmuch then as Christ hath suffered for us in the flesh, arm yourselves likewise with the same mind"*:. When you reach this mind set, then you are ready to have what God has promised to give his Folks. Brother Peter, assists our thinking, in showing us that this mind set is needed, since suffering is a guarantee.

In Romans 12:1-2, Paul tells us how we are to "Let this mind be in you(us), which was also in Christ Jesus." The text says, "*I beseech you therefore, brethern, by the mercies of God, that ye present your bodies a living sacrifice, holy, acceptable unto God, which is your reasonable service. And be not conformed to this world: but be ye transformed by the renewing of your mind, that ye may prove what is that good, and acceptable, and perfect, will of God.*" Paul indicates that the soul/person which does indeed allow God to take over his mind will enjoy the most overwhelming proof imaginable.   Such a state of mind is the highest destiny of mankind, being in perfect harmony with the good, acceptable and perfect will of God. God's way is the best way; his will is the perfect way for people; this mind set is acceptable and the soul/ person that tries it shall know that it is true. His own experience will demonstrate it, in the remainder of his/ her existence. His/her character will demonstrate it, as he or she walks among the world. His/her mouth will speak it, as he or she converse with the world. This mind set will most certainly produce evidence.

Now as we discussed earlier, this process takes some work that just might leave you with some scares, because it will most certainly be accompanied with pain as you go along. The words "living sacrifice" show us that some things have to be given up or left behind in order to present this acceptable sacrifice to God. Under the law, the sacrifices that were offered where dead, now it is with us under a better covenant of grace, we are to "present to God a living sacrifice." The sacrifices under the law, were offered upon an altar in which fire was involved. Under this new system of grace, the validity of our sacrifices that we should offer to God is manifested from the idea of us throwing ourselves on a burning altar. Which means that, there will be emotional, physical, mental, and even spiritual burnings that will cause some hurt. Just as it has already been discussed, "trouble doesn't last always," because strength is made perfect in weakness. It is with the believers' body that God is seen by those of the world. So when the mind has been changed by[1] the process of God, then the evidence will be seen in the body. The world does not have the ability to see God, so the evidence of God has to be shown in the lives of His children by the activities of the body. The cost that is involved in this offering our bodies to God, equals the "thorns in the flesh." Jesus said no man builds a house except first he sits down and counts the cost. The words of King David should provide us the ultimate understanding of the nature of this "living sacrifice" that we are to offer to the Creator of life. David said in II Samuel 24 : 24, "*neither will I offer burnt offerings unto the Lord my God of that which doth cost me nothing*" God wants us to know that we were worth the cost He paid for us, which should supply us with the assurance that He is worth the cost of us offering ourselves to Him.

The word "transformed" comes from a Greek word that brings us our English word metamorphose, which means that there must be and will be a complete change. When the world sees a man who was once a drug abuser now preaching, this is a noticeable metamorphism. This leads the world into a state of wondering how did this happen? When the world sees one who was full of hate now loving his neighbors, this is a noticeable change. Jesus says that if we have love one for another, then the world may know that we belong to Him. The actions of the body are governed by the mind, so this transformation happens when the mind is renewed. Here is again the reasons why the people of God should excel to the upper levels of spiritual perfection, emotional balance, mental assurance, domestic peace, martial harmony and even financial stability. Not that "gain is godliness," but when there is a visible and productive change in a believer's life, who is striving to be like Jesus, gain is partial and in many cases certain evidence of the transformation.

The "which is your reasonable service" brings to the mind of this author another phrase, which is "this is the least you could do." God wants us to present our bodies to him as a living sacrifice, which should be the least that we could do seeing that God _purchased_ our bodies(Acts 20 :28,1 Cor 6:19- 20). God simply wants what is His. The cost was a cost that we could not pay. The debt was too much for us to handle. God loved us so much(John 3:16), that he purchased us with His blood. This should serve as a motivational aspiration for us, to give God our bodies so that God can change our minds, so that we can understand the purpose of the pain that we go through as believers. The pain is to make us strong enough to get over the mountains of life and one day reach that holy city which God has promised to his folks. Once the mind is changed by God, then the spiritual life support depends on the service to God, which helps us to see the promise.

Chapter Four

Promise of God Moving In Your Life

II Peter I: 4, "Whereby are given unto us exceeding great and precious promises: that by these ye might be partakers of the divine nature, having escaped the corruption that is in the world through lust."

Promise is defined as an assurance that one will do something or that something will happen, or *"potential excellence."* Many of us in life have felt the trauma from being lied to by those whom we love. Many of us have experienced the blow of disappointment that followed a broken promise. We all were made to believe, as we grew up, that when someone says that they will do something, it will be done, only to find out, when we got older, that people have the ability to lie. We learned as we got older that not only do people have the ability to lie, but sometimes people are not able to keep a promise, even though they may have had intentions to fulfill it. Promises promotes expectations and expectations promotes dependency. When a promise is made, one expects the "promiser" to deliver and then a dependence is on that which was promised. Moreover, with all of that being true, there is one who cannot lie. There is one who has never made a promise that he could not keep. There is one whose nature is against anything that is associated with a lie. His name is Jehovah. His character provides valid expectations and dependencies, because He is known as a promise keeper. As Paul leaves Titus in Crete with those lying Cretians(Titus 1 : 12), he offers him comfort by telling him that the God of heaven cannot lie(Titus 1: 2). Seeing, that he had fulfilled His promise that He made before the world began, in delivering the world hope of eternal life through Jesus. With faith in Jesus, Titus could boldly do the work in Crete, despite the folks in Crete, because he recognized that God would always keep His promise.

PROMISED TO ABRAHAM

Despite the years of disappointing times in your life, you have to remain assured that God is able to do what you have been trying to do for years. As the Preacher would say, "when you have done all you can, then just let God do what you can't." God can do what you thought couldn't be done, He can change what you thought couldn't be changed, and He can fix what you thought was broken. Consider Abraham in this matter. Abraham and his wife Sarah were both well stricken in years. Both were in the realm of 100 years old and they did not have any children. In the Jewish society a woman who could not have children was basically considered nothing and a man who did not have a son wasn't too high on the "food Chain."

In a desperate attempt to give her husband a child, Sarah gave Abraham Hagar her handmaid; and in a desperate attempt to have a child, Abraham listens to his wife. God had made a covenant with Abraham to bless his seed(Gen 12: 7, Gen 15: 4) when Abraham was about 75 years old. God had promised to give Abraham a child "His way," but Abraham and his wife somehow lost their faith and their focus. Now here's where it gets interesting. In Genesis chapter 17, God commits to Abraham the covenant of circumcision. In the process, God changes Abram's name to Abraham(father of a great multitude) and his wife Sarai's name to Sarah(Princess). He tells Abraham that he and his wife would have a child, even in their old age and in verse 17, Abraham laughs. In chapter 18 at verse 12, Sarah laughs also to the news that they would have a child in their old age. God asks Abraham, "Wherefore did Sarah laugh, saying, Shall I of a surety bear a child, which am old?" God then ask and tells them in verse 14, *"Is any thing too hard for the Lord? At the time appointed I will return unto thee, according to the time of life, and Sarah shall have a son."* Now not only was Sarah old, but she was also barren, which means that normally she couldn't have had a child even if she was 20 years old. This unnatural occurrence would prove that, "there's nothing too hard for the Lord." God commands them that when the child is born call his name "Isaac," which means "Laughter." Now hear the sum of this matter, no matter how laughable a promise made by God would seem, God will always get the last laugh. Abraham laughed, Sarah laughed, but in Genesis 21 : 1-7, God gets the last laugh. This could be the very reason why Isaac means laughter/because there is nothing too hard for the Lord. God always keeps His promise. Now even though Abraham laughed and was old, he trusted that God was able to do what He said, seeing that he and his wife went through the process of having a child. Paul reminds us of Abraham's faith in Roman 4:16-21, *"Therefore it is of faith, that it might be by grace; to the end the **promise** might be sure to all the seed; not to that only which is of the faith of Abraham; who is the father of us all, (As it is written, I have made thee a father of many nations,) before him whom he believed, even God, who quickens the dead, and **calls those things which be not as though they were.** Who against hope believed in hope, that he might become the father of many nations, according to that which was spoken, so shall thy seed be. And being not weak in faith, he considered not his own body now dead, when he was about an hundred years old, neither yet the deadness of Sarah's womb: He staggered not at **the promise** of God through unbelief; but was strong in faith, giving glory to God; And being fully persuaded that, **what he had promised, he was able also to perform."** Just as God promised to bless Abraham and did, He'll do the same for us if we just believe and do as Abraham did. "Work like it depends on us, and believe like it depends on God." You might ask, "What has God promised me?" Well, God promised us the greatest gift ever and that's Heaven. Peter writes and says, *"Blessed be the God and Father of our Lord Jesus Christ, who according to His abundant mercy has begotten us again to a living hope through the resurrection of Jesus Christ from the dead, to an inheritance incorruptible and undefiled and that does not fade away, reserved in heaven for you."* This is the ultimate and awesome promise that God has given to us and has provided the way for us to get to it through Jesus. Moreover, He has also provided for us, through the Holy Spirit, the attributes to sustain ourselves while we live in this world(Gal 5 : 22 - 23). He has provide a continual cleansing process(I John 1 : 7). He has promised us that He would provide all our needs(Matt: 6: 25 - 34). He has promised us that He would even give us the desires of our hearts, provided we walk in His ways (I John 3 : 22). He has promised a greater return on what we have sown(Matthew 19 : 16 - 30 ; Luke 18 : 18 - 30: II Corinthians 9 : 6 -8)

Now before we leave this promise between God and Abraham, there is an element within that promise that we need not to overlook. Not only did God promise to give Abraham a son in his old age, but He also promised to bless the world through Isaac. God then commands Abraham to offer up Isaac to him for a sacrifice. The very one whom he was given as the result of the promise. To the carnal mind it would seem contradictory of God to have promised through Isaac countless descendant and yet at a time when Isaac did not have a wife nor child God commands him to be sacrificed. And if that was not profound enough, then notice that Abraham was more than willing to go through with the process. The secret to Abraham's willingness to offer up Isaac is seen in Hebrews 11: 17 - 19, which gives us an explanation for not only God's command, but also Abraham's obedience. For the Hebrew writer records these words, "By faith Abraham, when he was tried, offered up Isaac; and he that had received the promises offered up his only begotten son, of whom it was said, that in Isaac shall thy seed be called: accounting that God was able to raise him up, even from the dead; from whence also he received him in a figure." Every fiber of Abraham's being was wrapped up in the fact that God is able. Abraham trusted God even when the

49

instructions from God seemed unclear. We have to build this same kind of faith within our heart toward God, so that we can allow God to work wonders in our lives. God wants to bless us, so the question is how bad do we want to be blessed and not only that but, how bad do we want to one day see his face. The simple truth is this, in order for us to get to that city where the river flows with water of life, where there is a tree that is know as the tree of life, that we may freely eat from and live forever, we must develop this faith of Abraham. Notice that the Bible never gave levels of faith, but says, "without faith it is impossible to please God"(Hebrews 11:6).

Now if we look a little closer, there were a number of manifestations of Abraham's faith that could have lead God to stop Abraham from even going up on the mountain in the land of Moriah:

First of all, The fact that Abraham rose up early and **went** could have been enough to show God his faith. In Genesis 22 : 3, "So Abraham rose early in the morning and saddled his donkey, and took two of his young men with him, and Isaac his son; and he split the wood for the burnt offering, and arose and went to the place of which God had told him." Remember the ten lepers who came to Jesus asking for mercy and when the Lord instructed them to "Go show yourselves to the priests," Luke writes and says, "And it came to pass, that, as they **went,** they were cleansed(Luke 17: 11 - 14). Jesus tells the one who returned that his faith made him well.

Secondly, in Genesis 22: 5, we see why the Hebrew writer says that, "accounting that God was able to raise him up, even from the dead; from whence also he received him in a figure" Abraham tells the two young men with him that, "Abide ye here with the ass; and I and the lad will go yonder and worship, and **come again to you."** Abraham was telling them that he and Isaac would both come back down from the mountain alive. Surely that could have been enough to convince God of Abraham's faith.

Thirdly, in Genesis 22 : 7 - 8, when they reach the place commanded by God, Isaac notices that there is not a lamb for a burnt offering. Abraham's reply, surely could have been enough to prove his faith for he said, "My son, God will provide himself a lamb for a burnt offering."

Finally, also not only was Abraham's faith on trail here but we also see the faith of Isaac, who was old enough(between the ages of 25 - 33 years old) to have stopped his one hundred plus year old father from binding him to an altar and offer him up as a sacrifice. Genesis 22 : 6 and Genesis 22 : 8, both ends by saying, **"They went both of them together."** This shows not only Abraham's faith, but also the faith that he instilled within his son. This is why God would almost spare Sodom and Gomorrah for the request made to him by Abraham for God said in Genesis 18 : 19, "For I know him(Abraham), that he will command his children and his household after him, and they shall keep the way of the Lord, to do justice and judgement; that the Lord may bring upon Abraham that which he hath spoken of him." The fundamental fact of all of this is grounded in the fact that the same God that dealt in this fashion with Abraham is the same God that we serve today. The amazing question continues for blood washed believers, how could we live so far beneath our potential?

Paul tells the Galatian Christians, "Even as Abraham believed God, and it was accounted to him for righteousness. Know ye therefore that they which are of faith, the same are the children of Abraham   So then they which be of faith are **blessed** with faithful Abraham." (Gal. 3:6,7, 9). The blessings that will benefit the child of God are tied to faith and Jesus makes it clear that faith has no size, it only has influence. Which means that whether you are new to the faith or a 40-year veteran in the faith, it(faith) is the key to not only your blessings in this life, but also it is the vehicle needed to weather the storms of this life.

GOD'S PROMISE TO US THROUGH JESUS

Because of the pressure of Gnosticism(a heretical movement of the 2nd-century Christian Church, teaching that esoteric knowledge (gnosis) of the supreme divine being enabled the redemption of the human spirit.), John encourages his readers to hold to their faith in the Son of God. John says, in I John 2 : 24- 25, "Let that therefore abide in you, which ye have heard from the beginning. If that which ye have heard from the beginning shall remain in you, ye also shall continue in the Son, and in the Father. And this is the **promise** that he **hath promised** us, even eternal life." This is that promise that God made to bring man back to him. This promise that John refers to here is the promise of God performing reconciliation through a savior in the beginning when Adam and Eve fell in the garden. Sin entered the world and death by sin. Man became separated from God and there became a need then to bring man back to God. God made a promise to reconcile man back to fellowship and relationship with Him.   In Genesis 3 in the process of God condemning Adam and Eve for their transgression, he tells the serpent in verse 15, "And I will put enmity between thee and the woman, and between thy seed and her seed; it shall bruise thy head, and thou shall bruise his heel."   This would be the promise of the world receiving the Messiah. Now the question may arise, how can we see the promise of a savior in the text. If we look a little closer to the context of the text, the subject of the text is the seed. Which means a child would be born into the world to save the world from sin(Micah 5:2-3: Isaiah 9:6-7). Furthermore, the seed of the woman would some day defeat the serpent by crushing it underfoot, while he(the seed) would be bruised in the process(Isaiah 53 : 5). All of this points to Jesus, and this is that promise that John refers to in I John 2: 25, because when Christ rose from the dead he crushed the evil one(Rom. 16: 20; I Cor.15: 20 - 28). In Gen. 4: 1 -15, when Cain is born to Adam and Eve, it appears that she may have believed that he was the seed God had promised. Cain's name meant *Possession* and she noticeably gloated saying, "I have gotten a man from the Lord." Eve appeared to have been so taken with Cain that the other son was vanity or nothing to her. This is evident because Abel's name meant vanity. However this would not be the case, seeing that Cain turned out to be a murder and killed his brother Abel in a rage of jealousy.

Now, let us walk down the corridors of history, that is within the framework of the scriptures, so that we can see that the promise of the seed in Gen. 3:15 was indeed a promise made to those of us whom have been made the children of God, through the redemptive work of Jesus on

Calvary's hill. In Gen 12: 3, God said, "And I will bless them that bless thee, and curse him that curse thee: **and in thee shall all families of the earth be blessed.**" In Galatians 3, we see Paul affirms to his readers that the promise of all the world being blessed through the seed spoken of in the Genesis, is that of Jesus. Notice these words of Paul:

And the Scripture, foreseeing that God would justify the Gentiles by faith, preached the gospel to Abraham beforehand, saying, _In you all the nations shall be blessed._ So then those who are of faith are blessed with believing Abraham..... 13 Christ has redeemed us from the curse of the law, having become a curse for us (for it is written, _Cursed is everyone who hangs on a tree_), that the blessing of Abraham might come upon the Gentiles in Christ Jesus, that we might receive the promise of the Spirit through faith..... Now to Abraham and his Seed were the promises made. He does not say, _And to seeds,_ as of many, but as of one, _And to your Seed,_ who is Christ. And this I say, that the law, which was four hundred and thirty years later, cannot annul the covenant that was confirmed before by God in Christ, that it should make the promise of no effect. 18 For if the inheritance is of the law, it is no longer of promise; but God gave it to Abraham by promise. What purpose then does the law serve? It was added because of transgressions, till the Seed should come to whom the promise was made; and it was appointed through angels by the hand of a mediator..... For you are all sons of God through faith in Christ Jesus.....For as many of you as were baptized into Christ have put on Christ. There is neither Jew nor Greek, there is neither slave nor free, there is neither male nor female; for you are all one in Christ Jesus. And if you are Christ's, then you are Abraham's seed, and heirs according to the promise.

Can you see how God through the centuries of man's frailness, worked on our behalf to bring man back to Him? He kept His promise that he made to give the world a savior, despite Adam and Eve's fall, despite the continual flow of evil thoughts that where in the hearts of man in the days of Noah, despite the inability of Israel to maintain the Old Testament law. God worked through history and time to bring to pass that very thing that we needed to overcome this life so that we can reach glory. Jesus says in John 3:16, 17, *"For God so loved the world, that he gave his only begotten Son, that whosoever believeth in him should not perish, but have everlasting life. For God sent not his Son into the world to condemn the world; but that the world through him might be saved."* God loved us so much that he was willing to do whatever it took to get us back to him. Therefore, If we believed that Jesus is our redeemer, if we believe that God gave us that redeemer, if we believe that he gave us his spirit(Holy Spirit which works in us to change our character Gal. 5:22- 23), if we believe these facts, we ought to also believe that he can deliver us from the troubles in this life. We ought to be assured that God can get us through those storms that blow upon our marriages, our finances, our families, our jobs, and our health. We ought to be able to see ourselves on a continual march toward advancement. Paul tells the folks down in Rome in Romans 8:32, *"He that spared not his own Son, but delivered him up for us all, how shall he not with him also freely give us all things?"*

Don't let today just be "a day," but "the day" that you decide that your going to depend totally on God? Why don't you let this be the day that you will stop trying to use your strength and use His(2 Cor. 12:9). Make up your mind today, to stop defeating yourself with depression. Let yesterday be the last day that you will allow other folks to steal and kill your joy. Let yesterday be the last day that you will allow sin to take you farther than you were willing to go. Let yesterday be the last day that you allow sin to keep you longer than you wanted to stay and most certainly cost you more than your willing to pay. I came to realize that, Believing that God is able isn't the real problem, but the real problem is that we find it hard to allow him to do all that he is able to do. Here again is why Paul says in Eph. 3 : 20, "Now unto Him that is able to do exceeding abundantly above all that we ask or think, according to the power that works in us, ." Romans 16 : 25, "Now to Him who is able to establish you according to my gospel and the preaching of Jesus Christ, according to the revelation of the mystery kept secret since the world began." Jude 24, "Now unto Him that is able to keep you from falling, and to present you faultless before the presence of his glory with exceeding joy." He is more than able, so let today be the day that you will allow Him to move you into a greater position.

THE GOD THAT CAN'T MOVE

Have you ever told someone to stay put until you get back and when you got back they had left? Now if you where gone longer than expected, could you blame them for leaving? How long would you wait on someone, who told you to stay put until they got back? How long would it be until you decide to move? What about God? Have you ever wondered, does He move? Well, if you were wondering that, then the answer is no. Truth is, that not only does He not move, but He cannot move. The reason He cannot move is because it would be against His nature. Remember Titus 1:2, God cannot lie. With that being so, watch what God tells us through the Hebrew writer in Hebrews 13 : 5c, "For He Himself has said, I will never leave you nor forsake you." In other words, God is saying to us that He will not move. Even when trouble comes our way, He is still in the same place he was when his son was on the cross. So therefore, if there is any kind of severance between us and God, the move would come on our behalf. The only thing that can separate us from God is us(Isaiah 59: 1 - 2)(Romans 8 :, 35 - 39). Since he cannot and does not move, this should help us to know where He is in the mist of our troubles. The psalmist said in Psalms 46: 1, 11, "God is our refuge and strength, a very present help in trouble The Lord of hosts is with us; the God Jacob is our refuge." So from now on you should know that when you are going through those difficult times in life, God is right there with you, remember the poem of "footsteps." God does not move.

There is another awesome aspect in the fact that God doesn't move. It is seen in the parable of the prodigal son in Luke 15: 11 - 32. Jesus shows us in this parable God's amazing position. Both sons were lost. One was lost while gone and the other was lost while still at home. Now watch how God dealt with both sons while staying in the same position. When the son that left home finally came to himself(Luke 15:17), he comes back to his father and repents. Now notice where the father is as the son is returning home in Luke 15: 20, "And he arose, and came to his father, But when he was yet a great way off, his father saw him, and had compassion, and ran, and fell on his neck, and kissed him." Notice that when he(son) was a great way off, his father saw him. The father, who is representative of God, was still in the same place he was, when the son, who is the representative of us, left his house. The same love the father had for the son was also still there, even to the high extent, that when he returned it was time to rejoice(Luke 15: 22 -5). Even if and when we leave God, even when we separate ourselves from the Father of life, He and His love is still in the same place it was when we left. When the children of God leave and then return home, God rejoices (Luke 15: 7, 10, 22 - 25). Here is also a good lesson for the church as a whole, to rejoice when a brother or sister repents and returns back to God. Which takes us to the other lost son, who never physically left, but was gone while still at home. The eldest son was upset because of the rejoicing over the younger son who had returned. He was so bothered by this that he wasn't willing to participate in the rejoicing. Notice the position of the father, "*And he was angry, and would not go in; therefore came his father out, and entreated him. And he answering said to his father, Lo, these many years do I serve thee, neither transgressed I at any time thy commandment; and yet thou never gavest me a kid, that I might make merry with my friends; But as soon as this thy son was come, which hath devoured thy living with harlots, thou hast killed for him the fatted calf. And he said unto him, Son, thou art ever with me, and all that I have is thine. It was meet that we should make merry, and be glad: for this thy brother was dead, and is alive again; and was lost, and is found.*" The eldest son was lost at home, because he had disowned his brother(**But as soon as this thy son was come**) even after he had repented and returned home. So the father had to remind his eldest son that even though the younger son had left and wasted his living on harlots, he was still his brother(*It was meet that we should make merry, and be glad: for **this thy brother** was dead, and is alive again; and was lost, and is found*).

The sensational truth of this subject of God not moving is that not only should we know that he'll be there in the midst of our trouble but he'll also be there if or when we fall, leave him, get back up and need to return to him. The Proverb writer says, "For a just man falls seven times, and rises up again"(Proverbs 24 :16). Now some would ask, "how can a man be called "just" if he falls so many times?" He is just because he knows that the Father is still in the same place he was in before he fell, which gives this "just man" the motivation to keep on getting up. Also, we have to come to the compassionate understanding that since God is a present help for us, he is also a present help for our brothers and sisters when and if they fall. So we should have, compassion on them and not want to disown them just because they have failed, but render a helping hand to pull them out of that miry clay. The essence of our duties to our brothers and sisters, once we become spiritually strengthen, as seen in Luke 15, is that when a member of God's family leaves, our duty is to go and retrieve. If we can't retrieve, then if and when they return we must be willing to receive (Gal 6:1-5).

When "God's folks" reach that level of spiritual understanding that God will keep His promise, then all of us who have confessed our faith in Him, will stay where He is, no matter what tries to move us, seeing that we know that "he will never leave us nor forsake us"(Hebrews 13:5). When we reach that spiritual level, to see God for who He is, then we can and will, allow Him to move in our lives because when we let Him move, then we will not move(II Peter 1 : 10). Paul told the Colossians, "And you, who once were alienated and enemies in your mind by wicked works, yet now He has reconciled in the body of His flesh through death, to present you holy, and blameless, and above reproach in His sight-- if indeed you continue in the faith, grounded and steadfast, and *are not moved* away from the hope of the gospel which you heard, which was preached to every creature under heaven, of which I, Paul, became a minister._(Col. 1: 21 - 23). Paul tells Corinth, "Therefore, my beloved brethren, be steadfast, **immovable**, always abounding in the work of the Lord, knowing that your labor is not in vain in the Lord."(l Cor. 15: 58). If God can't move, we have to find it within ourselves to stay put, even in our crushing circumstances.

THE GOD THAT CAN'T QUIT

For most people, it is a frustrating thing to see someone not finish something they started. Even for many it is a difficult thing to start a task and then for some reason or another not finish it. But when we consider God in this matter, it is a certainty that God will not start something that he will not complete. The reason for this is found within the fact that God cannot lie, but He has to keep His promise(Hebrews 6 :13- 18). The fact that He never moves also provides for us evidence that He will always finish what He starts. Whatever is connected to God, whatever come out from God, will accomplish its goal. For example, God wants his children to be holy in all manners of our life(I Peter l: 15). The reason we have to be holy is because "without which no man shall see the Lord"

(Hebrews 12: 14). Holiness is only produced through the word of God, as was discussed earlier. ,God gave us His word so that we would be able to "see the Lord." That word that was produced from the mind of God was sent here so that we could have the same mind as Him(Phil. 2 : 5). Notice that God tells Israel through Isaiah that His word was going to accomplish what it was sent to do; *"Let the wicked forsake his way, And the unrighteous man his thoughts; Let him return to the Lord, And He will have mercy on him; And to our God, For He will abundantly pardon. For My thoughts are not your thoughts, Nor are your ways My ways," says the Lord. "For as the heavens are higher than the earth, So are My ways higher than your ways, And My thoughts than your thoughts. _For as the rain comes down, and the snow from heaven, And do not return there, But water the earth, And make it bring forth and bud, That it may give seed to the sower and bread to the eater, So shall My word be that goes forth from My mouth; It shall not return to Me void, But it shall accomplish what I please, And it shall prosper in the thing for which I sent it"* (Isaiah 55: 7 - 11). Now here's the sum, Israel had forsaken the ways of God and God allowed them to go into a Babylonian captivity for 70 years. In Isaiah 55 God gives them an invitation to return to Him and leave their wicked ways. He shows them here that man's ways and thoughts are merely nothing and destructive unless they are traded in for God's ways and thoughts. God began a prestigious work in establishing Israel as a great nation. He made a promise to bless the world through Abraham and to bring the world a Savior through the loins of David and this would come to pass regardless of what would happen.

When we look to the New Testament, we see this same thought given to blood washed believers in II Tim. 3:15-16; "*All scripture is given by inspiration of God (or God breathed), and is profitable for doctrine, for reproof, for correction, for instruction in righteousness: that the man of God may perfect thoroughly furnished unto all good works .*" God intended for His creation of man to be perfect and good, which shows us why he has not given up on man. Therefore, whatever condition you were in when you came into Christ, God intends to make you better. Whatever has your mind stressed out, God intends to make your burdens lighter. It has always been God's intentions to have people that the world could see through and see Him. To accomplish this, God has to work on us until it's time for us to leave this life. Ephesians 2:8-10, "For by grace are ye saved through faith; and that not of yourselves; it is the gift of God; Not of works, lest any man should boast. For we are his workmanship(craft), created in Christ Jesus unto good works, which God hath before ordained that we should walk in them." We are his handy work. He is the potter and we are the clay(Romans 9: 21). Therefore, some of the changes that you are experiencing in your life right now are do to the fact that God is working on *you*. Some of the people that have moved away from you and left you are do to the fact that God is working on you. The reason why your tastes for certain things have nearly become unnoticeable, is do to the fact that God is working in your life to get you ready for the day of Jesus Christ.

To gain a better understanding of this work that God preforms on his children in order for us to be ready when Jesus comes, here's what Paul would tell us in Phil. 1: 6 "Being confident of this very thing, that he which hath begun a good work in you will perform it until the day of Jesus Christ." Now, there are four things in this verse that we need to see: There's a **Divine Commencement, a Divine Commitment, a Divine Completion,** because of our **Divine Connection.**

DEVINE COMMENCEMENT

Phil 1 : 6 "Being confident of this very thing, that he which hath **BEGUN.**" God started this work in and on you. The only thing you had to do with it was except it. Eph. 2 : 8, "For by grace are ye saved through faith; and that not or yourselves; it is the gift of God; Not of works, lest any man should boast." God started this because he knew just what to do to get us away from the dark and deadly state that we were in.

DEVINE COMMITMENT

Phil 1 : 6 "Being confident of this very thing, he that which hath begun a good work in you **WILL PERFORM IT.**" God's going to finish what he started, which means that he's not going to give up on you like most folks would. God will even work through our faults to bring to pass His purpose in us, remember David and Bethsheba(II Samuel 11 - 12).

DEVINE COMPLETION

PHIL. 1: 6 "Being confident of this very thing, he that which hath begun a good work in you will perform it **UNTIL THE** day of Jesus Christ" God will finish this work no matter what. Every word, that comes from the mouth of God has to obey His lips. So He must finish this work that He began in you to make you better in the future than you where when you came to Him.

DEVINE CONNECTION LEADS TO A DEVINE COMPLETION

John 15 ; 5 "I am the vine, ye are the branches: He that abides in me, and I in him, the same brings forth much fruit; for **without me ye can do nothing."** The only way God cannot finish this work on you is that, if you break the connection with Jesus. However, because of this connection God is able to work on us, in us, and through us to perform His operations. Now that we are connected to Jesus there isn't much that we can not do. Because of this connection Paul could say, **"I can do ALL things** through Christ which strengthens me." (Phil 4: 13). Notice that with the connection we can do "ALL THINGS." Without the connection we can do "NOTHING." Looking at this work that God has started on us and seeing his commitment to finish it, should help us to be confident in the words of Romans 8: 31b, "if God be for us, who can be against us." Our spiritual life has to be filled with the thought that if other folks are not happy with whom I am then all they have to do is wait, because God isn't through with me yet. People in this life have a snapshot mentality when it comes to your past mistakes. Some people just will not allow you to forget nor get past that thing you did years ago, whether it was to them or they just know you did it. But God has a video camera mind where he records, not only what you did, but what you have done to rectify that mishap. Also, just like a video camera has the ability to delete something, God will also delete your past mistakes. When it has been deleted by God we ought not to allow others to affect us with it. God cleans and God forgives, and that's all we need to be concerned about not what man has to say. God has the last say so and that is why He is a God that can't quit.

The ground work of a promise is solidified, not by the words of the promise but by the character of the one who made the promise. Because of God character, we know that He will keep His promise. We are His top priority, because when one is concerned about bringing what he promise to pass, he will make fulfilling that promise His top priority. God has promise to be there for us. Therefore, we ought to stop worrying about things we cannot change and allow God to give us the strength to change those things that we can change.

CHAPTER FIVE

Privilege of Partnership

ONE OF THE GREATEST BLESSINGS that we have within the Body of Christ is that we are not in this battle of life alone. Not only is God always with us and has promised us that He will never leave us, the Great Almighty formulated a support team, called "the body" or Church. It is a beautiful thing to know that we have a team of believers that God has assembled together for the purpose of assisting one another in this conflict of spiritual warfare. When your finger is hurting on your physical body, your whole body experiences the pain also. Therefore, this same idea applies to the spiritual body. We have a spiritual team and just as it is with any team, the goal is that the team works together to achieve a victory. "Together Each Achieves More," is said to be the meaning of the word team and when we develop a greater understanding of this concept, this concept would then lead us into a well-nourished level of maturity in the area of having all things common. Notice how the scriptures teach this factor in Acts 4 :

32, "Now the multitude (Church) of those who believed were of one heart and one soul; neither did anyone say that any of the things he possessed was his own, **but they had all things in common."** Paul tells the believers in Philippi, "Let nothing be done through selfish ambition or conceit, but in lowliness of mind let each esteem others better than himself. Let each of you look out not only for his own interests, but also for the interests of others(Phil. 2:3-4). The mighty theme in the New Testament seems to be rooted in the fact that we, all believers, are in this together. Which means that we should weep together, we should hurt together, and we most certainly should rejoice together. God has given us help not only in heaven, but also here on earth. Paul tells those in Rome, *"Let love be without hypocrisy. Abhor what is evil. Cling to what is good. Be kindly affectionate to one another with brotherly love, in honor giving preference to one another; not lagging in diligence, fervent in spirit, serving the Lord; rejoicing in hope, patient in tribulation, continuing steadfastly in prayer; distributing to the needs of the saints, given to hospitality. Bless those who persecute you; bless and do not curse. Rejoice with those who rejoice, and weep with those who weep. Be of the same mind toward one another. Do not set your mind on high things, but associate with the humble. Do not be wise in your own opinion if it is possible, as much as depends on you, live peaceably with all men"(Roman 12: 9 - 16, 18 NKJ).* In this portion of theses writings we shall see through the eyes of the scriptures, the amazing truths of us not having to go through trouble alone. We shall even see, that we don't have to try and fight the devil alone, but work together to bring defeat to him and victory to the "team."

I'LL WATCH YOUR BACK

The devil is a very sneaky and crafty being who will stop at nothing in trying to bring down the children of God. Therefore, we have to be ready "lest Satan should get an advantage of us," for we cannot be ignorant of his devices. He will attempt to lead us into sin with the idea that God will forgive us and once we have given in to sin, he'll try and convince us that what we have done was too bad for God to forgive. One of my instructors in ministry said once that, "the devil doesn't have a problem with you, but his problem is with God, and since he cannot touch God, he tries to bring down the closest thing to God and that's God's children." In Rev 12:10, Satan is called an "accuser," which means that he looks to bring accusations against the children of God. Now despite the fact that he is the father of lies, this would be the only time he tells the truth, when he accuses. God has deemed his children as a holy nation, a royal priesthood, a peculiar people, chosen, conquers, and when we fall, commit sin, the devil brings the accusation to God hoping that God would inflict the punishment of death that was said to be the result of sin(Ezekiel 18 :4, Romans 6 : 23, James 1: 15). He accuses, to throw in the face of God, all that God has called us and it is as if he says, "I thought you said he was holy, and if he is holy then why did he sin?" The devil wants to completely destroy you and what better way to do it than by the hand of your Creator. But God is able to give mercy at the same time, he administers judgement, all because of what took place on Calvary's hill. So the devil is mad because you left him and he wants you back. Remember when you were out in the world, how it seemed as if you had fewer troubles as you do now. Well the simple truth is that you were in the hands of Satan, you were in his house, and he is against messing with his own house. Now if that didn't set well with you then, look at what Jesus said when He was accursed of casting out demons by the power of Beelzebub, *"Every kingdom divided against itself is brought to desolation, and every city or house divided against itself will not stand. If Satan casts out Satan, he is divided against himself. How then will his kingdom stand?"* (Matt. 12 : 25 - 26) Therefore Satan does not mess with those in his house as he does those of God's house, simply because he wants to keep them in his house.

Since he is a meddler, a manipulator, and a menace to all that is Godly, he's always looking for opportune times to attack God's folks(Luke 4:13). As a matter of fact, he always attacks from behind or when you least aspect. Which means, he never shows up in front of you or he never shows the destruction of what he offers, but appears as a "wolf in sheep's clothing"(II Cor. 13-15). He shows the deceptive splendor of sin, but never the destructive splinters that one would reap from sin. Peter tells us that he does this by waging his attack on us from the blind side or the back. Be sober, be vigilant; because your adversary the devil walks about like a roaring lion, seeking whom he may devour"(l Peter 5 : 8). Peter warns the believer that the devil is just as a lion who hunts for prey, he sneaks in and before you know it, he pounces on you and tries to catch you with your guards down. Whenever the enemy wants to gain a decisive advantage over his victim, he tries to hit 'em from the blind side, which most of the time is in the rear. Now here's the sum, Peter goes on to say in I Peter 5 : 9, _Resist him, steadfast in the faith, knowing that the same sufferings are experienced by your brotherhood in the world." So therefore, as much as it may seem, Satan is not just at you but he is also after the entire brotherhood and sisterhood of believers. Being that the scriptures provide for us evidence that Satan is at us all, this proves more of a reason why we are Privileged with Partnership. We have a charge of watching another's back. All of us have a blind side and because we have that blind side, we have to watch that blind side for each other.

The question now becomes, how is this done? The answer is found in Paul's letter to the church of the Ephesians. Paul writes and tells the saints in Ephesus that in order to stand against the wiles or trickery of the devil, they and all those whom have confessed their faith in Christ must put on the whole armor of God. Paul shows that unless we have our loins or waist gird about with truth, unless we put on the breastplate of righteousness, unless we have our feet shod with the preparation of the gospel of peace, unless we have our shield of faith, we can not quench those fiery darts of the wicked. Unless we put on that helmet of salvation and carry the sword of the spirit, which is the word of God, we can not handle the devil. This is the spiritual equipment that our "commander and chief" has supplied for us in this spiritual war. This armor serves as our spiritual defense against the devil and his wicked workers called principalities, powers, the rulers of the darkness of this world, and the spiritual wickedness in high places. These wicked workers are the agents who serve as the role of antagonist in this spiritual battle we are engaged in and this armor serves as the strength needed to stand against these demonic forces. Now when the understanding comes, that each of us must put on this armor, there comes also the knowledge of understanding that this armor you have put on is not just for you, but you have it on for your brothers and sisters in the faith as well. Watch what Paul goes on to say in Eph. 6:18, "praying always with all prayer and supplication in the Spirit, **being watchful to this end with all perseverance and supplication for ALL THE SAINTS.**" Now watch the break down of this:

ALL kinds of prayers and supplications are to be used: public prayers, private prayers,intercessory prayers, prayers of thanksgiving, every kind. Not just for yourself, but also forall saints.

ALL seasons are the season of prayer: all times of the day, all conditions andcircumstances, all occasions, all states of mind, etc. Even in the mist of his trouble, Jobprayed for his friends.

ALL perseverance: through times of discouragement or defeat when it seems that all islost, when victory has gloriously smiled or when it has cast a deemed frown .... let nothinghinder your life of prayer.

ALL the saints are to be remembered in prayer. Here's where the rubber meets theroad, we have to intercede or go to God on behalf of our brothers and sisters, simplybecause when the devil hurts one, he hurts many. Sometimes all it takes is one bad apple to spoil the whole bunch. Sometimes if he hits the right one, that one can affect the body in a very disastrous way. Just like an infection in your baby toe, can cause death, if it's not takencare of, that one in whom the devil and his wicked workers get a hold of, can cause adeadly infection to spread throughout the church. Look at what Jesus says about the onewho has been infected by these wicked workers in Luke 11 : 24 - 26, "When an uncleanspirit goes out of a man, he goes through dry places, seeking rest; and finding none, he says, I will return to my house from which I came.' And when he comes, he finds it swept and put in order. Then he goes and takes with him seven other spirits more wicked than himself, and they enter and dwell there; and the last state of that man is worse than the first." Looking at what the devil and his wicked workers are able to do, this, should help all of us in the body to sympathize with why it is an overwhelming need to watch out and pray for one another.

Even though the Christian has put on the whole armor of God, he cannot win the victory except through a constant reliance upon prayer. A Believer that chooses not to pray, is like a man who chooses not to breathe, he soon will die. It is said that the Roman warriors would fight back to back in battle, because the armor they wore was stronger and mainly in the front, which left the back areas expose. The same image is projected to us, with this spiritual armor, as we battle together in this spiritual warfare. We must stand back to back and fight together.

I'LL HELP YOU CARRY YOUR LOAD

Galatians 6 : 1-5, "Brethren, if a man is overtaken in any fault, ye which are spiritual restore such a one in a spirit of gentleness, considering thyself lest thou also be tempted. Bear one another's burdens, and so fulfill the law of Christ. For if a man think himself to be something, when he is nothing, he deceives himself. But let every man prove his own work, and then shall he have rejoicing in himself alone, and not in another. For each one shall bear his own burden."

Regardless of your social, ethnical, financial, geographical status all have burdens. All have a heavy load that they must bear, especially those of the household of faith. So as it has been discussed in these writings God's folks, are not immune to suffering. Burdens are sure things in this life that come sometimes when we least expect them. Some of us have experienced the burden of unexpected financial issues, after the death of a loved one, or a horrible accident, or a sudden sickness in a child. Burdens are also sometimes filled with unbearable weight. So with them possessing such heavy weight, we are taught through the scriptures on how to handle these burdens. The scripture shows us that burdens have a slight difference and therefore must be handled in three different ways. First and foremost there are some burdens that just get too hard to bear, so therefore we should take them to the Lord and leave them there(Psalms 55 : 22, 1 Peter 5 : 7). Then we are taught, by the scriptures, that there are burdens we must bear on our own(Gal. 6 : 5). Moreover, since we have the Privilege of Partnership in the faith, there are some burdens that we are commanded to share with one another. Hence Paul's letter to the Galatian Christians, who were being persuaded to hold on to portions of the law of Moses. For this section, a good understanding of these burdens will be appreciated by a breakdown of the Gal. 6:1-5 texts:

The setting of this letter that Paul writes to the Churches of the Galatian Believers, surrounds the fact that there was a group of folks who had come into the church, who were known as Judaizing Teachers. They were teaching the believers over there that except you keep certain aspects of the law of Moses, such as circumcision, then you could not be saved. As Paul brings this letter to a close, he teaches on the characteristics of the Holy Spirit and he shows how one would walk when he or she is walking in the Spirit. He then gives the one who is Spiritual an understanding that they have a duty to all those in the family of God(Gal 6 : 10). He shows those who have grown to a spiritual level of maturity that there are some in the body who have been "hit from the blind side" or overtaken by a heavy burden and they need help to carry and support their load. The only ones whom Paul would recommend to help those who had been overtaken, would be those who had built themselves up spiritually enough to help or restore somebody else. Now what is meant by "overtaken"; **Overtaken = Greek _Prolambano, _** which means to be taken before, to anticipate, to forestall to take one by forestalling (him, i.e., before he can flee or conceal his crime). When the word is broken down, the meaning becomes clearer: **Pro = Before & Lambano - being taken or to be caught off guard.** This word suggests that one can be caught off guard by the devil before they know it. However, the major issue with being caught off guard is that one may lose sight on how to get back or in most cases(with those who haven't grown spiritually) unable to pick themselves up out of darkness, unable to carry their load. Unfortunately there are times when our spiritual family members fall and we need to be there to help them up in the spirit of meekness. Which would mean, when you have develop spiritually, then you have within you the right kind of instrument to play away that bad spirit that has overtaken the one whom you are trying to restore(I Samuel 16 : 23). The Holy Spirit lays the proper words on your tongue, so that you are able to say the right words to comfort the one who is burden by the troubles of this life. The Holy Spirit has guided you down the right paths of life which has given you the experience needed to help your brother/sister with their heavy weight.

Now here's where this dazzling benefit of having fellow soldiers in this spiritual warfare comes in. The word "burden" in Gal 6 : 2 is from the Greek word Baros, which means a heavy load. It suggest the idea that life handed down issues that are sometimes just too heavy for one to endure by themselves. This word gives us a picture of one struggling to carry a very heavy object and trying to carry it a great distance and is experiencing trouble carrying it alone. Paul teaches the believer here, that in order for us to "fulfill the law of Christ," he or she is obligated to assist with that heavy load. Moreover, these words of the Apostle Paul even transcend the idea of more than just helping one up who has fallen. He shows us here that we must also get under their load with them and help them go the distance. The overall idea is that there is a weight pressing down on you, caused by the issues of life, caused by the abandonment of a spouse, caused by the lost of your job, causes by folks in the church, and according to the law of Christ, I am responsible for getting under that heavy weight with you and we together bear that burden as long as it takes. Hallelujah, in the name of Jesus, how good it is to know that we are privileged with a partner, so that we don't have to go "thru" alone. So if you're in a situation that seems just too heavy to bear, and you've been trying to give it to God, but for some reason when you leave talking with God, you take it back with you, then just call that one person who you believe to be spiritual enough to help. Believe it or not there are many in the church who are spiritual and are willing to help.

Now, here's why I am obligated to help you carry your load. Paul says, "considering thyself lest thou also be tempted." In other words, I have to remember that there was a time when I didn't have everything together and there was a time when I needed someone to help me carry my load. There was a time when I was not spiritual, and now that I have reached the point and process of spiritual grow, I don't need to be Pharisaic. That means, that I don't need to walk around and act like your sins are bigger than my sins. I don't need to walk around with my nose turned up in the air and looking down on you. My father in the gospel, Lee Otis Smith, Sr, would often say, "when you point one finger at someone else, you always have three pointing back at you." Here's why Paul could go on to say, "For if anyone thinks himself to be something, when he is nothing, he deceives himself." Those who are pretenders in the faith, have only themselves fooled by acting like defenders of the faith. Therefore, stop trying to carry that weight of depression, of financial struggles, of abandonment, of ridicule from folks in the church by yourself. God has prepared someone close to you to help you with your struggle. Paul proves this in Gal. 6 : 5, "For each one shall bear his own load." Now as contradicting as this may seem, Paul is not opposing what he had just said about each of us bearing one another's burden. He teaches here, that it is the responsibility of each member of the body to participate in burden bearing. The word "Burden" in Gal. 6: 5 is from the Greek word, Phortion (for-tee-on), which gives reference to "one's own duty." The metaphorical idea is that of a solider having to carry his own pack, just as all in that troop. If one part of the body of Christ refuses to help pull the weight of another part of the body's load(Burden _Baros_), then they are refusing to pull their own weight. They are refusing to perform their duties(Burdens _Phortion_) as a Child of God. Surely

God is more than able to provide for us help with these conflicts in life. Surely, there are members of the body who are "real" and not playing church. You do have brothers and sisters in the family who are willing to suffer with you as long as it takes, to gain a victory together. When one wins, we all win, and just the same, when one loses, we all suffer from that lost. Don't worry about those members of the body, who will not help, just know that there are members of the body whom God has prepared that will.

SUMMARY

The Sum of the Whole Matter

ONE OF MY FAVORITE SONGS is "Love lifted me." It's one of my favorites because I can see myself in the lyrics. The song goes, "I was sinking deep in sin, far from the peaceful shore, sin so deeply stained within, sinking to rise no more, but the Master of the sea, heard my despairing cry, and from the waters lifted me, now safe am I. Love lifted me, love lifted me, when nothing else could help, love lifted me." Can you see yourself in this song? The mighty Master ministered to my misery and made me move to a place of peace. I am so ever indebted to the Master of life, that I just believe that I owe him my life. Every thing in life isn't always clear, but one thing is certain for me, and that is God is able. When Jonah was drowning for his own faults, God already had a great fish prepared for his deliverance. That same God that delivered Jonah, those three Hebrew boys from the fiery furnace, the children of Israel from the bondage of Egypt. He is just as able today as He was then. That's the God that I have come to know.

Even in my imperfection He keeps on loving me and leading me in His ways. He gave me this Position, He gave me this Power, He gave me this Purpose, He gave me that Promise, He blessed me with Partners so that I could one day be with Him in Glory. I have learned to stop waking up in the morning and wondering how I got up. I have learned to stop wondering how I made it through dangers seen and unseen. I've stopped wondering how God has put up with me and all my messes. I've stopped wondering how, because I found that it was Grace that brought me this far and Grace will lead me on. So now when I wake in the morning, I no longer ask how, but why? Why did God wake me another day? Why did God save me? Why did God take an old wretch like me and place me into the ministry? The answer that God has given me to "why" is because I have been given a Purpose to show the world that I believe God's Promise in His word, and I have become filled with Power to show the world God by my Position by helping and loving my Partners in the faith.

My dear friend, my fellow believer in the kingdom, we must fulfill our destiny and walk in the light of Christ. We must put to bed all those excuses for not living up to our full godly potential. It's time for us to deny the devil and his wicked workers their victory over us. We are royalty, we are chosen, we are more than conquers. There is no weapon, that the devil can create, that is powerful enough to remove us from the hands of God. Unfortunately, we have that ability to do it to ourselves. Don't let your life become a repeat of Israel in the wilderness. Aren't you tired of being defeated? Aren't you tired of not being able to see the sun because of the clouds? Allow this to be a new day. Allow this to be the beginning of your walking in the light of God's favor. We all have issues to face and to get over. Yet when you take a closer look at your issues, you'll find out that your issue sounds like "it's you." You have the power to reach a higher dimension. You have the power, because of your position, to live with joy and peace. Despite the fact that he or she left you. Despite the fact that your struggling with money. Despite the fact that your struggling with sickness, you are His child. Jesus says this to you today, "shall not God avenge his own elect, which cry day and night unto him, though he bear long with them." God has your back, to keep you from going back, so now is the time to stop looking back and look to Jesus who is the author and finisher of our faith(Hebrew 12 : 2). My life's scripture is Psalms 40: 1-3, "I waited patiently for the Lord; and he inclined to me, and heard my cry. He also brought me up out of a horrible pit. Out of the miry clay, and set my feet upon a rock, and established my steps. He has put a new song in my mouth- Praise to our God; many will see it and fear, and will trust in the Lord." I received an email once that really helped my spirit when I was feeling down. It was entitled, "The wooden bowl." The story was touching, but the ending was soul stirring. The email ended by saying, "On a positive note, I've learned that, no matter what happens, how bad it seems today, life does go on, and it will be better tomorrow. I've learned that you can tell a lot about a person by the way he or she handles four things: a rainy day, the elderly, lost luggage, and tangled Christmas tree lights. I've learned that, regardless of your relationship with your parents, you'll miss them when they're gone from your life. I've learned that making a "living" is not the same thing as making a "life." I've learned that life sometimes gives you a second chance. People love that humans touch — holding hands, a warm hug, or just a friendly pat on the back. I've learned that I still have a lot to learn. God is able and He is life. The sooner we learn this, the better we will become. This is a proper perspective for peculiar people's pathway to perseverance. We are God's folks.

Printed in the United States
110094LV00001B/49-57/P